KILIMS

KILIMS
A BUYER'S GUIDE

Lee Allane

With 88 illustrations, 43 in colour

Thames and Hudson

Acknowledgments

I would like to express my gratitude to David Aaron (Aaron Gallery, London), Hans Christensen (Bickenstaff & Knowles, London), Nash Dan (Anglo Persian Carpet Company, London), Paul Garrod (Chandni Chowk, Exeter), Guri Le Riche Eastern Artifacts (Edinburgh), Rosalind Price (Chandni Chowk, Barnstaple), Ron Stewart (Liberty, London), Iain Scott-Stewart (Rippon Boswell, London) and Sam Wennek (Chairman, Rippon Boswell International) for their considerable help and advice on kilims and other flatwoven artefacts. Thanks are also due to Glynis Bell, James and Enid Bell, Garth Cartwright, Tony Franks, Alastair Hull, Yvonne Manning and Dorota Zdzienski for allowing me access to their excellent private collections. I must also acknowledge the contributions of Dori Zdzienski, whose multi-lingual talents eased the complexities of translation, and Douglas Robertson whose photographic services defied the twin challenges of weather and rail strikes to ensure that every kilim was photographed. And finally a very special debt of gratitude must be extended to Andrew Daws and Hannah Lewis for their hard work and diligence in producing the superb illustrations and original photographs used in this book.

I must also acknowledge the courtesy and cooperation of Liberty PLC, The Anglo Persian Carpet Company, and Messrs Chandni Chowk and Guri Le Riche Eastern Artifacts for supplying the majority of kilims and flatwoven items contained in this book.

The sources of the photographs of the colour plates are as follows: Hannah Lewis 2–9, 11–18, 20–24, 26, 28–37; Anglo Persian Carpet Company 1, 39–42; Douglas Robertson 10, 19, 25; Alastair Hull 27, 38.

The sources of the kilims that appear in the plates are as follows: Liberty PLC, Regent St, London, and provincial branches 5, 7, 9, 11, 13, 14, 16, 17, 22, 23, 30, 35; Chandni Chowk, 1 Harlequin, Paul St, Exeter, and 45 Boutport St, Barnstaple, Devon 2–4, 6, 15, 18, 21, 24, 34, 36, 37; The Anglo Persian Carpet Company Ltd, 6 South Kensington Station Arcade, London 1, 39–42; Guri Le Riche Eastern Artifacts, 3 Upper Gilmore Place, Edinburgh 19, 25; The private collections of Glynis Bell 12, 32, 33; James and Enid Bell 26, 29; Garth Cartwright 8; Tony Franks 10; Alastair Hull 20, 27, 38; Yvonne Manning 31; Dorota Zdzienski 28.

Line drawings by Andrew Daws
Original photography by Hannah Lewis

British Library Cataloguing-in-Publication Data

A catalogue record for this book is available from the British Library

ISBN 0-500-27841-5

Printed and bound in Hong Kong by Mandarin Offset

Contents

How to use this book

The range and variety of kilims on sale in a dealer's showroom, a shop or a department store can be overwhelming, especially as items of very similar appearance and quality are often sold for vastly different prices, and you may feel totally at the mercy of the salesman. *Kilims: A Buyer's Guide* has been systematically organized to answer all your immediate questions, as well as to provide a comprehensive introduction to the subject.

IF YOU ARE A COMPLETE BEGINNER, turn to Chapter I, which will explain *what kilims are*; *how they get their names*; and *where and by whom they are made*, as well as providing an explanation of the *essential kilim-making terms*. There is a brief history and a detailed breakdown of how *kilims are classified*, according to their *country of origin, weaving group and weaving category*. Chapter II tells you *how kilims are made* and how the different *techniques, tools and materials* affect their character, quality and appearance, as well as explaining the *dyeing process* and the *meaning and origin of colours*. It also provides detailed information on *traditional kilim shapes and sizes* and a variety of *special kilims, bags and artefacts*.

You will now have a grasp of the basics and should feel confident enough to consider BUYING A KILIM. Turn to Chapter III, which will help you choose *the right kilim at the right price*, whether you want it as an investment or simply as something to enhance the decorative impact of your home. It explains how to avoid paying too much, or buying something totally unsuitable for your needs, and helps you to assess *quality, suitability and value for money* by providing a detailed guide to *relative prices* and *where and when to buy or sell*, as well as useful information on the *care and repair* of your kilim.

IF YOU WANT TO KNOW MORE about a kilim you already own, or simply expand your knowledge of the subject turn to Chapter IV, which provides background information on the CULTURAL CONTEXT in which kilims are produced. This will help you unravel the complex, and often frequently changing, interrelationship between the weavers and the countries in which they live. The information has been methodically organized for easy reference under clear headings which relate to *the major ethnic and cultural groups*, the various *cultural and religious influences* that have helped form their weaving heritage and the diverse effects of successive *invasions, migrations and empires*.

Further in-depth information on the *origin, meaning and cultural dispersal of kilim designs* is contained in Chapter V, which, in addition to providing a fascinating insight into the various weaving cultures, will also help in identifying the possible origin of kilims from different parts of the weaving region.

Detailed information on the WEAVING NATIONS, TERRITORIES AND REGIONS is contained in Chapter VI, and has been organized to give an easy cross-reference between the *ancient and contemporary weaving regions*, including a detailed breakdown of the *former Soviet Caucasian and Central Asian Republics*, as well as information on the quality, design, colours, size and type of the *general contemporary workshop kilims* that are currently being produced.

Finally, Chapter VII contains a complete guide to *tribal, regional and contemporary weaving groups*, arranged alphabetically for easy reference. This provides detailed information on quality, design repertoire, colour schemes, price, size and type of kilims produced by each weaving group, which will further expand your knowledge of the subject.

Clear cross-references and headings, supplemented by a thorough index, allow you to follow any line of enquiry by moving easily through the text and referring to the *maps and line drawings*. *Colour plates* – each chosen to illustrate a particular design or type of kilim currently available – offer instant visual examples to supplement the information provided in the text.

CHAPTER I

What is a kilim?

The term 'kilim' is commonly used to describe any flatwoven (pileless) rug, regardless of its design, weaving technique or place of origin. However, the term is more properly applied only to those items, produced using a number of flatweaving techniques, that share a common (predominantly Islamic) design heritage and originate from a broad geographical corridor stretching westwards from North Africa and the Balkans, through Turkey, Iran, Afghanistan and the southern republics of the former Soviet Union, to Pakistan and China.

A number of different names are used by the weavers in certain countries to describe their flatwoven rugs – *gelim* in Iran, *palas* in the Caucasus and *chilim* in Romania. In the West, though, we normally use either the Afghan word *kelim* or, more frequently, the Turkish *kilim* as a collective term applied to items from any of the producing countries.

The flatwoven rugs produced in India (known as *dhurries*) have their own distinctive design and weaving heritage and so are generally thought to belong to an entirely separate tradition. This is also true of traditional flatwoven items produced in other parts of the world – for instance, Navajo rugs from North America, textiles from Africa and native Indian weavings from Mexico, Peru, Ecuador and other parts of South and Central America – which, regardless of any similarities in weaving technique or design, are not normally referred to as kilims.

Authentic kilims can be defined, therefore, as flatwoven rugs produced by a number of weaving techniques (*see* Chapter II) originating from a specific geographical area (*see* Map 1) and conforming to a broad, but nonetheless distinctive, design heritage. (*See* Chapter V)

Kilims and pile rugs

The term 'oriental rug' can be applied both to kilims and to pile rugs, although, in practice, many dealers make a distinction – referring to pile rugs as oriental rugs and flatwoven rugs as kilims. However, kilims and pile rugs originate from the same geographical region and both are made by the same ethnic groups and share a common cultural and design heritage. The most obvious difference between the two is the weaving technique.

Kilims are produced by interweaving individual warp (vertical) and weft (horizontal) strands of material in such a way as to create the rug's physical structure and the design visible on the front. The exact nature of the design is determined by a combination of the colours of the individual warp and weft strands, and the specific weaving technique. (*See* Chapter II)

Pile rugs, in contrast, are made by tying, or knotting, small ribbons of individually coloured material (which form the pile) around the warp strands and then using the weft strands to hold them in place. The design is not created by the colours of the warp and weft strands or by the specific weaving technique, but by the juxtaposition of each individually coloured ribbon of pile. (*See* Chapter II)

It is generally believed that pile rugs evolved from flatwoven rugs and that they were first made when a weaver inserted pile material into a kilim foundation to make it thicker, warmer and more durable. It would be a mistake, however, to view kilims as simply primitive, less sophisticated versions of pile rugs. Kilims have maintained a parallel tradition that is arguably more faithful to their common weaving heritage and, in terms of skill and artistry, has consistently produced items that compare favourably with the finest pile rugs.

Kilim terms and names

There are several terms, names and expressions commonly used by kilim dealers that may be unfamiliar to those who are relatively new to the subject. Most will be explained fully in the appropriate chapters, but there are a few that need to be clarified at the outset.

Rugs, carpets and runners Terms used to denote size and shape – a carpet being a rug whose surface area is more than 4.4m² (47 ft²) and whose length is less than 1½ times its width, i.e., 9' x 6' (2.74 x 1.83 m). This distinction is generally only made in Britain and the British Commonwealth and is usually applied solely to pile rugs. Occasionally a dealer will refer to a 'kilim rug' or 'kilim carpet', but more often than not they will simply call any flatwoven item a kilim, regardless of its size. Runners are long, narrow rugs – normally their length is 2½ times their width – and kilims with these dimensions are often referred to as kilim runners.

Spelling and pronunciation

Spelling Varies considerably for place names, kilim names and terms because the spoken languages in most of the kilim-producing regions employ written scripts (e.g., Arabic) whose alphabets do not correspond directly to those used in the West. Consequently, most translations are strictly phonetic.

Common variations in spelling are too numerous to list, but it is useful to remember that the following letters are often interchangeable: 'q' and 'k', and 'i' and 'y' (e.g., Qashga'i, Kashga'i or Kashgay); 'a' and 'e' (e.g., Belouch or Balouch); 'a' and 'eh' (e.g., Senna or Senneh); 'o' and 'u', and 'j' and 'g' (e.g., *khorjin* or *khurgin*); and sometimes 'g' and 'k', and 'e' and 'i' (e.g., gelim or kilim). There is no discernible rationale behind any of these variations and, as yet, there seems to be little desire in the trade to assist the consumer by trying to unify variant spellings. To ascertain whether an unfamiliar name may be a variant spelling, repeat it (preferably out loud).

Certain combinations of letters not usually found together in English or other European scripts (e.g., 'gh', 'kh', 'qa', etc.) may be used to indicate a specific sound that does not have a direct phonetic translation – the modifying consonant ('h') is frequently omitted in some words (e.g., Kazakh/Kazak or Kirghiz/Kirgiz), but rarely, if ever, in others (e.g., Bakhtiari).

Pronunciation Generally fairly straightforward: each syllable is given equal emphasis (e.g., Bakhtiari is pronounced 'Bakh-ti-ar-i' and Taimani 'Tai-ma-ni'). Some vowel and compound consonant sounds (e.g., 'gh' and 'kh') are totally alien to anyone other than a native speaker, but small mistakes in articulation rarely present a problem, even in the producing countries, because most dealers are familiar with Western modes of speech. Similarly, most of the modifying consonants – such as 'h', which adds a slightly elongated guttural stress to the preceding letters, usually 'g' and 'k' – can be largely ignored. The letter 'q' is roughly equivalent to the English 'k' and the names Qazvin and Aimaq can therefore be pronounced 'Kazvin' and '*Aimak*' without running the risk of being misunderstood.

How kilims get their names

Place of origin or tribe In common with oriental rugs, kilims are traditionally named after their place of origin or, in the case of nomadic items, the weaving tribe. For example, an item made in the Iranian (Persian) town of Senneh is known as a Senneh and one produced by the nomadic Belouch tribe is called a Belouch.

Place of origin and tribe Both are sometimes used to indicate that a kilim was produced by weavers from a tribe (or tribal group) inhabiting one particular area, rather than by members of the same tribe living elsewhere. For instance, if a kilim is marketed as a Kerman Afshar it implies that it was made by the Afshar tribesmen living around the town of Kerman, in south-east Iran, as opposed to the Afshar who inhabit the Azerbaijan or Khorassan regions in the north-west and north-east of the country. This practice is normally applied only if there is a discernible difference between items produced in each region and if there is clear evidence of the kilim's exact origins.

Double tribal name Sometimes used to show that a kilim was produced by a sub-tribe of a larger tribal grouping. For example, a Yomut Turkoman was made by the Yomut branch of the Turkoman ethnic-linguistic group; and a Maldari Belouch was produced by the Maldari, a sub-tribe of the Belouch. Again, this practice is normally only employed when there is a clear indication of an item's exact origin, otherwise it will be marketed under the more general tribal name.

The name of the design or weaving technique May be used if a more exact attribution is unclear. For example, the *mir* or *boteh* design is employed by a number of weaving groups, so if an item cannot be given either a tribal or regional attribution it may simply be marketed as a *Mir* kilim. Similarly, a kilim woven in the *soumak* technique may be marketed simply as a *Soumak* if its origins are totally obscure or as a Russian or Iranian *Soumak* if only its country of origin is known.

The name of the marketing centre Tribal kilims, in particular, are sometimes named after the town where they are collected and marketed. Towns such as Shiraz in southern Iran and Bokhara, in Turkmenistan, have for centuries acted as centres for a number of nomadic and semi-nomadic tribesmen, who sell their wares and buy supplies in the towns' bazaars. It became common practice for Western importers to name any item emanating from these (and other) market towns after the town itself, rather than the weaving tribe. Today, dealers usually make a greater effort to obtain a more specific attribution, but where this is not possible kilims are still sold under the name of the town in which they were traditionally marketed.

Generic names Sometimes used when a more specific attribution is not known. For example, the town of Zarand, in northern Iran, lends its name to kilims produced both in Zarand itself and also to items that conform to the general style associated with a broad area encompassing the towns of Qazvin and Saveh. Also certain contemporary workshop kilims may be produced from more than one location and are also sold under generic names, e.g., Hanbel, Oudzem, etc.

Range names A number of major retail outlets (department stores, etc.) also market contemporary workshop kilims under so-called range names that bear no relation to where or by whom they were made.

The relationship between names and weaving groups Kilim names are usually synonymous with their classification into weaving groups, i.e., an item made by the Belouch nomads would normally be called a Belouch and would be classified as belonging to the Belouch weaving group. However, kilims named after their design or weaving technique (e.g., a *Mir* or a *Soumak*) may belong to one of several different weaving groups and unless the term is prefixed by the name of a specific weaving group (e.g., a Senneh *Mir* or a Shirvan *Soumak*) you can assume that the actual weaving group is unknown.

A brief history

Flatwoven rugs of some kind are produced by cultures throughout the world and it is impossible to trace the origins of flatweaving to any specific source. Many of the weaving techniques used in kilim production are almost identical to those employed to make clothes and decorative tapestries, as well as flatweaves produced in other parts of the world. It seems probable, therefore, that the skills of flatweaving, in common with those of pottery and painting, evolved independently in various places at different times. Kilims, as we understand the term today, however, belong within a specific historical and cultural context that shares its evolution and traditions with pile rug weaving. It is therefore necessary to discuss the history of oriental rug weaving as a whole and then trace the slightly different evolutionary paths taken by kilims and pile rugs.

The origins of oriental rug weaving are obscure. Their raw materials (wool, cotton and silk) are naturally perishable and can only survive for a few centuries, unless kept under extraordinary conditions. Consequently, the vast majority of old and antique items still in existence were made during or after the 18th century. This makes it virtually impossible to chronicle their exact evolutionary development and dispersal throughout the oriental-weaving region.

The theory most generally accepted – by both historians and dealers – is that all oriental rug and kilim weaving stems from Central Asian or possibly Mongolian nomadic cultures. Certainly, the nomadic lifestyle (as migrating herdsmen) not only gave them ready access to the raw materials, but also necessitated the use of multi-functional and easily transportable 'furniture and furnishing'. This theory was reinforced, in 1947, when a Russian archaeologist, S. J. Rundenko, discovered a Scythian (or possibly Turkoman) tomb – located in the Altai Mountains in southern Siberia – containing a number of flatweaves (or kilims), felt rugs and a hand-knotted carpet that had been preserved almost in its entirety. The tomb had been broken into shortly after it was sealed, allowing water in, which subsequently froze during the Siberian winter, miraculously preserving the contents for over 2,000 years.

The Pazyryk carpet (as the hand-knotted carpet is known) and the other textile fragments have been dated to around the 5th century BC and represent what many historians believe to be the earliest examples of authentic oriental pile rugs and kilims – strengthening the theory that weaving originated in Central Asia.

If this theory is true then it is reasonable to assume that the various nomadic tribes (Turkic and Mongolian) gradually spread their weaving skills throughout the entire weaving area – partly through trade, migration and intermarriage and partly as a result of their numerous conquests and invasions. We know that Kublai Khan (1215–94), who founded the Yuan (or Mongol) dynasty in China (c. 1279–c. 1368), encouraged Mongol, Turkic and other nomadic weavers. Similarly, the Seljuk, Ottoman and other Turkic-speaking tribes, who established empires in Asia Minor, the Caucasus, the Balkans and the Middle East, brought with them their rug-making skills and, no doubt after absorbing and refining native weaving traditions, elevated kilim and pile rug weaving into a major artform and means of cultural expression.

The exact pattern of dispersal is unknown, but it is clear from a combination of physical and historical evidence that oriental rug weaving has existed, in some form, throughout the entire weaving region, for at least 3,000 years. Fragments of flatwoven material, dating from the beginning of the 1st millennium BC, were discovered in excavations as far apart as Mongolia and Turkey. Some of the earliest examples (dating from the 7th to the 11th centuries BC) were found in Fostat, near Cairo in Egypt.

A number of other textile fragments, woven using kilim weaving techniques and spanning a time-frame from the 1st millennium BC to AD 1500, have also been discovered in Turkey, Mongolia, Siberia and other parts of the weaving region. However, it is not always clear which of these examples were intended for use either as clothes, or tapestry decorations, or as flatwoven rugs.

In addition to concrete physical evidence, there are also a number of historical, literary and pictorial references that point to a flourishing kilim and pile-rug weaving tradition, stretching from Greece through Central Asia into eastern China, which was in existence from at least the late 2nd century BC and probably dates back even further.

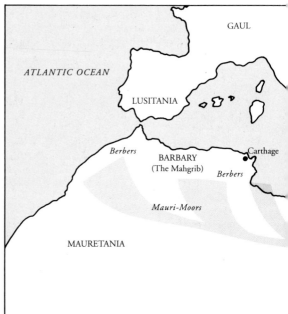

Top: weaving region with current national boundaries

A divergence of traditions Evident at a very early stage in the weaving evolution between items that are either essentially tribal or workshop in character, appearance and origin. Each of these two broad categories has its own particular characteristics, qualities and appeal and can be seen as a direct continuation of two distinct, parallel traditions whose origins can

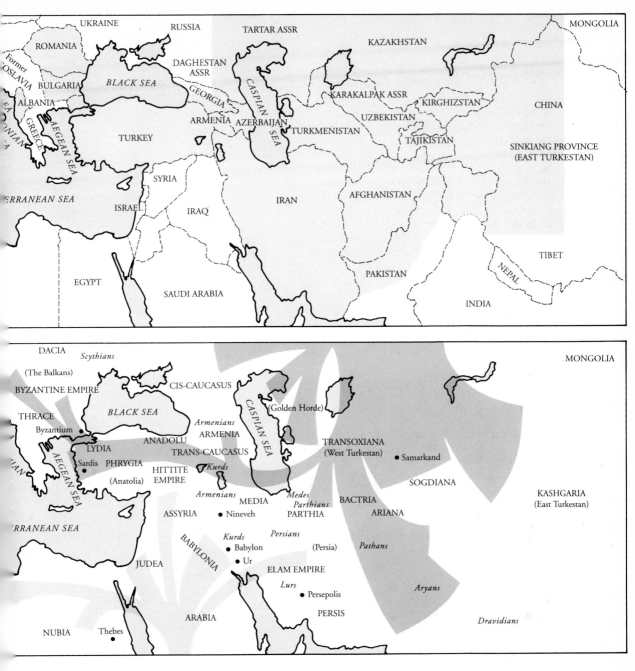

Above: weaving region between *c.* 500 BC and AD 1500. The Turko-Mongol invasion/migratory routes are dark grey and the Arab invasion/migratory routes are light grey

arguably be traced back to at least the 1st millennium BC. The Pazyryk carpet – with its relatively high knot count and sophisticated, partly naturalistic, design – seems more appropriate in a royal palace than on a nomad's floor and shows a definite divergence from the more primitive and functional contemporaneous tribal weavings. We also know from chroniclers that both tribal and more sophisticated 'court' kilims and pile rugs were being produced during the Sassanian Empire in Persia (*c.* 224–*c.* 641); and the Chinese Sui Annals (510–617) mention a huge, probably flatwoven, carpet – called the Spring Carpet of King Chosroes – found in the King's palace at Ctesiphon, which was reported to be 'brocaded with gold and silver threads and inlaid with jewels and pearls'. However, it is not until the 15th and 16th centuries that a clear division between these two parallel traditions begins to emerge.

The tribal tradition Seems to have remained relatively faithful to early Central Asian and other nomadic weavings, typified by the use of bold, mainly geometric designs, strong colours and an emphasis on the character, vivacity and functionality of the rug, rather than its technical or visual sophistication. Certainly we know from studying surviving kilims and pile rugs – as well as, for example, the paintings of Holbein (*c.* 1497–*c.* 1543), which often include rugs in the background – that tribal weaving has changed little over the last few centuries. Today it continues to be produced by Turkoman, Belouch and other nomadic and semi-nomadic people, in addition to a number of settled tribal groups in villages and smaller towns – primarily in Iran, North Africa, Afghanistan, Pakistan and Central Asia.

The workshop tradition Probably has its origins in one of the Middle Eastern or Central Asian civilizations that flourished between the 1st millennium BC and the 1st millennium AD (Assyrian, Achaemenian, Sassanian, Scythian, Turkoman, Mongolian, etc.). But, it is impossible to trace a continuous evolutionary pattern until the 15th and 16th centuries when the Safavid Shahs (in Persia), the Ottomans (in Anatolia) and the Moghuls (in India) controlled their respective empires. They established workshops and encouraged the most accomplished weavers to produce incredibly intricate and sophisticated items that would serve to show off the wealth and splendour of their rule. Many of these 'court' carpets, as they are frequently called, were later imported into Europe by the royal houses, and by the aristocracy, wealthy merchants and landowners, inspiring the creation of the Aubusson and Savonnerie workshops in France and the production of the magnificent floral and heraldic European-style court carpets woven in Britain, Ireland, Italy, Poland, Spain, Romania and other parts of Europe between the 16th and 19th centuries. The European carpet weaving industry was more or less totally mechanized by the end of the 19th century (except in Ireland where the superb hand-knotted Donegal carpets are still produced). Some of the designs used in the old European-style court carpets are now found in the modern Chinese Aubusson or Peking range of handmade pile carpets and (usually in a more simplified form) in a number of contemporary workshop kilims – mainly from Turkey and the Balkans (e.g., Sarkoy, Bessarabian).

The Oriental-style court carpets, produced during the 15th and 16th centuries, are direct antecedents of the more sophisticated items made in numerous urban workshops throughout the rug-producing world. Although these contemporary workshop items were generally smaller and less ornate than their predecessors – in keeping with Western decorative requirements – they nevertheless follow the court tradition, not only in their overall structure and design, but also in their emphasis on technical perfection and virtuosity.

The evolution of kilims and pile rugs Kilims have largely stayed within the tribal tradition and most of those on the market today are still essentially tribal in origin, appearance, character and methods of weaving. However, a number of countries are now producing contemporary workshop kilims, which, while frequently tribal in appearance, have been modified – in both design and methods of production – to satisfy Western decorative requirements. Pile rugs, in contrast, have diverged more evenly into both traditions, resulting in a vast range of equally accomplished tribal and workshop rugs and carpets, although the trend has been increasingly towards workshop production, resulting in fewer authentic tribal items finding their way to the West.

Collecting kilims This is a relatively recent development in the West and, although a few dealers and collectors have had a long-standing enthusiasm, it was not until the 1960s – when Westerners became interested in Eastern cultures and began travelling in increasing numbers throughout the weaving regions – that kilims began to make a substantial impact on Western markets. Many of these so-called 'sixties travellers' brought kilims home as souvenirs and some went on to establish collections or open shops selling kilims and other ethnic artefacts. These new collectors, unlike their predecessors in the 15th and 16th centuries (who specialized in pile rugs), were more interested in kilims as examples of the weaver's uncorrupted cultural heritage, rather than as opulent and prestigious furnishings. Over the next few decades, as the interest in kilims increased, there was a gradual recognition by dealers and producers that these 'inferior' items – previously held in such low esteem that they were frequently used as the outer wrappings on bundles of pile rugs – were an untapped source of profit and trade. They not only extended the range of items available for existing pile rug markets, but also appealed to people who had previously shown little interest in oriental rugs. At the same time, kilim designs were also making a considerable impact on Western furnishings and began to appear with increasing regularity on a wide range of fabrics used for clothes and furnishings.

Public collections Substantial public collections of kilims are largely limited to the former Soviet Union – particularly in the Museum of Ethnography and the Russian Museum, St Petersburg (formerly Leningrad), the Museum of Azerbaijani Carpets and Handicrafts, Baku, the Makhachkala Art Museum, Daghestan, the Museum of Georgian Architecture and Daily Life, Tbilisi, and the Museum of the History of Armenia, Yerevan (Erivan) – although several museums in the West have a small number of items on display. This relative scarcity of public collections is primarily because very few kilims were exported to the West (in comparison with pile rugs) until the latter half of the 20th century; and many museum curators shared the same general disregard for kilims that was prevalent in the producing countries.

Classifying kilims

There is no single, comprehensive or universally applied criterion for classifying kilims. Centuries of migration, conquest and cultural exchange have ensured that few producing countries can claim a totally independent ethnic or weaving heritage. National boundaries have also changed dramatically, sometimes dividing homogeneous ethnic groups; and, even today, the borders and ethnic mix of some producing countries are far from stable and both may change during the next few decades. It is not surprising, therefore, to find that many of the kilims made by Kurdish tribesmen, for example, have more in common with the kilims produced by their kinsmen living in other countries, than they have with the items woven by their non-Kurdish neighbours. There is also often a closer affinity between Kurdish tribal kilims and those produced by non-Kurdish tribal groups than between Kurdish tribal kilims and those made in urban workshops by people of Kurdish descent. Similarly, workshop kilims made in different countries are frequently closer, in character and appearance, to each other than to local tribal kilims.

It is therefore necessary to employ several criteria when classifying kilims – the most important of which are: country of origin, weaving group and weaving category – and also to recognize that the importance or even relevance of each criterion may vary in accordance with the specific nature or origin of different items. For example, some modern workshop kilims are not marketed under any tribal, regional or even generic name, and so only need to be classified according to their weaving category and country of origin. However, an additional 'weaving group' classification is required for workshop items made in the same country but marketed under different generic names (e.g., Oudzem and Tiffelt kilims from Morocco) because they are made to separate standards of manufacture, appearance and price. However, there is no point in trying to give them a tribal or regional classification because their character and appearance is not dictated by the weaving traditions of a specific location or weaving tribe. In contrast, it is essential to employ an additional ethnic criterion when classifying Moroccan kilims produced by the Beni Quarain and Oulad Bou Sbaa tribes because they represent Berber and Arab weaving traditions respectively, and failure to take this into account will undermine the connection between their kilims and those produced by other Berber and Arab weaving groups.

Country of origin

It is both logical and necessary to classify all kilims according to their country of origin because production costs, exchange rates and import/export tariffs and regulations may vary considerably from country to country, resulting in wide price discrepancies between items of comparable quality, depending on the importing and exporting countries involved. The political situation in each producing country, and its relationship with individual importing nations, may also affect the availability of certain items. There is usually some degree of uniformity in the overall character and appearance of items made in the same country, although the dramatic changes in national boundaries, the divisions of people of the same ethnic group across two or more borders, and the diverse cultural, ethnic and religious backgrounds of the current inhabitants, make it impossible to place all the kilims produced in each country into one homogeneous category.

In order to limit the degree of confusion that these factors may cause, a detailed breakdown of the major ethnic groups and the current and traditional names of the weaving nations and territories are contained in Chapter VI.

Weaving groups

The term 'weaving group' is normally applied to any village, town, geographical region or tribal group that produces kilims that combine both an ethnic or a regional connection with an overall uniformity of weaving structure and design. The term can be applied either generally or specifically.

It is common practice to classify all kilims and oriental rugs according to a sliding scale of attributions, based on the degree of certainty about their actual origins. Consequently, a kilim will normally be classified progressively as being Iranian (country), north-west Iranian (region), Azerbaijan (province), Heriz (conurbation) or Mehriban (weaving village). Mehriban – and to a lesser extent Heriz – would be considered the specific weaving group and Azerbaijan or north-west Iran the general weaving group.

Normally kilims are sold under the names of their specific weaving groups when their exact origins are known and under the name of a more general weaving group when a more precise attribution is unclear. (*See* How kilims get their names, p. 8)

Both character and origin should be considered when defining a weaving group. An ethnic or regional connection on its own is not enough – the kilims must also conform to a broad uniformity of structure and design. For example, ethnic Arabs produce kilims in a number of different areas of North Africa, Turkey and Iran, but they are not considered to form a general 'Arab' weaving group, despite

having the same ethnic origin. This is because the items made in each of these areas are often closer in structure and appearance to other localized weavings than to Arab kilims produced elsewhere. In contrast, Turkomen tribesmen weave items in a number of countries which, allowing for some regional and sub-tribal variations, possess sufficient similarities to be classified as belonging to the same general weaving group. However, it is not uncommon for towns or regions to produce some items that conform to a local or regional style, and others that do not. For example, the town of Bergama, in western Turkey, has a history of kilim and pile rug weaving stretching back to at least the 16th century and items made in the town have been traditionally marketed as belonging to the Bergama weaving group. In recent years, however, Bergama has also become a centre for the production of contemporary workshop kilims, which are based on a wide range of modern and traditional designs from different parts of the kilim-producing world, and which cannot properly be said to belong to the Bergama weaving group. Consequently, the traditional items woven in the town are considered to be products of the Bergama weaving group, and the non-traditional items should be marketed under the broader category of contemporary workshop kilims. (*See* A localized diversity of weaving groups, p. 15)

General weaving groups Can be defined as having a strong regional or ethnic connection, combined with an overall uniformity of weaving style, but also containing a number of smaller weaving units (e.g., villages, sub-tribes, etc.) whose items, while staying within the overall stylistic framework, retain their own individual variations. For example, the Belouch are a large, homogeneous tribal grouping whose traditional territory stretches from eastern Iran, through Afghanistan into west Pakistan. They are composed of a number of nomadic, semi-nomadic and settled sub-tribes and splinter groups, who weave their own distinctive kilims and rugs. However, despite the diversity of their locations, lifestyles, sub-tribal allegiances and weaving styles, Belouch kilims as a whole are seen as being sufficiently uniform in character and appearance to justify being considered part of a general weaving group. The same criteria can also be applied to Turkoman, Kurdish,

Shahsavan, Luri and a number of other large ethnic or tribal groupings.

Similarly, kilims from certain urban centres and regions are also seen as possessing sufficient stylistic uniformity to be viewed as forming a general weaving group. For example, the area around the town of Hamadan, in western Iran, contains dozens of small villages that produce items which, despite their individual nuances, conform to a collective Hamadan style and can therefore be said to belong to the general Hamadan weaving group.

Specific weaving groups Can be defined as individual weaving units (e.g., villages, tribes or sub-tribes) that produce their own distinctive kilims and may or may not be part of a much broader, general weaving group. For example, the Maldari, a sub-tribe of the Belouch, produce their own distinctive kilims which can be classified as belonging to both the general Belouch weaving group and to the more specific Maldari (or Maldari Belouch) weaving group. Similarly, an item originating from the village of Tuisarkan, near the town of Hamadan, in western Iran, belongs to the specific Tuisarkan weaving group, but may also be classified as being part of the general Hamadan weaving group. In contrast, the Iranian towns of Senneh and Bidjar are not usually considered to be part of a more general regional weaving group because their items – although sharing some collective characteristics – are not sufficiently akin to those produced in neighbouring villages.

A localized diversity of weaving groups More than one specific weaving group may co-exist in the same location. For example, the Iranian Province of Azerbaijan is noted for producing items from a number of specific weaving groups – some of whose products conform to an overall Azerbaijan style and some of whose do not. Similarly, some towns have their own local weaving tradition and also act as marketing and distribution centres for a number of totally independent tribal weaving groups whose kilims may or may not bear any resemblance to those produced in the town itself. For example, Veramin, in northern Iran, is populated by ethnic Afshars, Kurds, Lurs and Persians – as well as Shahsavan and other tribal confederations – whose individual weaving traditions have been eroded by centuries of settlement, intermarriage and cultural osmosis resulting in a collective Veramin style. However, Veramin still acts as a marketing centre for nomadic and semi-nomadic tribes in the region and some settled tribal groups still produce items that are sufficiently distinct as to warrant classification as 'specific' weaving groups. Consequently, Veramin is the centre for both its own kilims, which are usually marketed as Veramins, and also tribal kilims normally marketed under their tribal name (e.g., Shahsavan or Shahsavan of Veramin).

Sometimes, however, there is no discernible difference in the outward appearance of items produced by a tribal group and those made by non-tribal weavers in the marketing town. For example, kilims made in the town of Shiraz, in southern Iran, by a mixture of ethnic Qashga'i, Lurs, Arabs and other racial groups normally look exactly the same as those woven by the Qashga'i, Luri and Khamseh nomads who migrate throughout the region and it is not always possible, even after a close examination of the materials and weaving technique, to make a more specific attribution. As a general rule, if there is any doubt about whether or not a kilim is of tribal origin, it should be marketed under the name of the town (e.g., Shiraz) rather than the tribe (e.g., Qashga'i), but this practice is not always followed.

The relationship between kilim and pile rug weaving groups Some weaving groups (e.g., Senneh, Belouch and Shahsavan) produce both kilims and pile rugs to an equally high standard and normally employ a similar range of designs and colour schemes. However, a number of weaving groups (e.g., Mut, Fethiye and Maimana) make only kilims, or so few pile rugs that they should be discounted as a pile rug weaving group, and many of the most famous pile rug weaving groups (e.g., Isfahan, Kashan and Hereke) rarely, if ever, make kilims. As a general rule, the weaving groups who follow the workshop tradition tend to specialize in pile rugs, whereas the tribal weaving groups (whether nomadic or village) are more likely either to produce both or to concentrate mainly on kilims.

Weaving categories

The weaving category to which an item belongs relates to its overall character and appearance, rather than to where or by whom it was made. In kilim weaving the main categories are tribal, regional and contemporary workshop. A number of weaving groups produce kilims that clearly belong to only one of these categories, whereas others may produce a greater diversity of work, some of which may cross over into an adjacent category. There are also a few groups whose general output straddles the border between two categories and could easily be placed on either side. However, both the criteria applied to determine the category and the categories themselves are by necessity somewhat arbitrary and should be viewed as a useful means of simplifying the broad trends in kilim production, rather than as being hard and fast classifications.

Tribal kilims (pls 2, 10, 36, etc.) Produced by nomadic and semi-nomadic tribesmen (semi-nomads spend part of the year in villages or settled camps) and by settled people, usually in villages and small towns, who have retained much of their original tribal identity and weaving heritage and whose kilims still possess a distinctive tribal character and appearance.

The nomadic lifestyle is ideally suited to kilim weaving. Most nomads are herdsmen who need to migrate to follow the natural cycle of available pasture, water and shelter. This provides them with an abundant supply of wool and the other raw materials needed for weaving – cotton as well as indigo, madder and many other plants used for dyeing are frequently endemic to their migratory routes. It also ensures a socially stable division of responsibility between 'men', who tend the herds and protect the tribal unit, and 'women', who maintain the household and make most of the artefacts and wares that the tribe need both for personal use and for trade.

The physical environment in which most nomads live has a profound effect on the character, appearance, size and shape of nomadic kilims. Their traditional territories often encompass vast tracts of semi-desert or mountainous terrain where sudden climatic changes are common, making it extremely difficult for them to predict whether or not their seasonal pasturelands and watering places will be adequate when they actually arrive. It is therefore essential for their continuing survival that they maintain a degree of flexibility in their movements and have the capacity to break camp, find alternative pastureland and establish a new encampment in the shortest time possible. High mobility is partly achieved by living in *yurts* (round tents, usually made of felt or

goatskin stretched over a wicker frame) and partly by having 'furniture and furnishings' that can be assembled easily and quickly, taken down and reassembled. Kilims play their part as floor coverings, tent flaps, blankets, table cloths and a wide variety of storage bags and other functional artefacts that cannot only be packed and unpacked quickly, but are also relatively lightweight and convenient to transport. However, the nomadic lifestyle and environment places a number of physical and compositional limitations on the type of kilims they can produce.

The size and shape of nomadic kilims, for instance, is largely determined by the type of loom used for each individual item. Nomadic tribes rarely spend more than a few months in any one place and their kilims have to be woven from start to finish during that period or fastened to the loom and transported in their unfinished state to the next encampment. This makes it impractical for them to weave large, carpet-size items – which are unlikely to be finished before the next move – because transporting the heavy, vertical looms necessary to weave these items would be extremely difficult, if not impossible, depending on the distances involved and the severity of the terrain. Consequently, during their migrations, the nomadic tribes normally use relatively lightweight and easily transportable horizontal looms (sometimes little more than four pieces of wood secured to the ground by pegs), which restrict the weaver to producing something that is only as wide as she can reach across from the sides without losing her balance or control. Vertical looms are sometimes employed during periods of extended settlement, allowing larger and wider carpet-sized items to be produced, but the vast majority of authentic nomadic kilims are either relatively small or long and narrow.

The nomads' designs are also both restricted and inspired by their lifestyle and environment. The physical constraints placed upon the weaver, the limited availability of dyes and materials and the need to preserve the underlying functionality of their weaving combine, with a more general artistic and cultural expression, to create the unique character of nomadic designs. These kilims are typified by the bold simplicity of their compositions, the vibrancy of their colour schemes (whose entire effect is sometimes achieved with only three or four primary hues) and the use of mainly angular, sometimes purely geometric, motifs and shapes. Curvilinear designs are rare and many forms, which may have been derived originally from plant or animal sources, are now so abstracted that they may be considered purely geometric. Even forms that are clearly recognizable as people, animals and plants are invariably articulated with the sharp, angular contours needed to harmonize with the overall geometric nature of the composition. One of the most important and characteristic features of nomadic kilims is the frequent inclusion of powerful totemistic elements (usually of plant or animal origin), ranging from specific identifying tribal insignia (e.g., *guls*) to a variety of talismen aimed at warding off the evil eye. Whether today's weavers are fully aware of the significance of these symbols or whether they have simply become subliminal elements in the tribe's repertoire of designs, is a matter of considerable debate, but there is no doubt that they add to the overall character, vitality and mystique of nomadic weaving.

Women are responsible for the weaving in all nomadic cultures. Young girls are taught the skills from childhood and it is normal practice for them to display their early solo works as part of their rite of passage into womanhood and eligibility for marriage. Gradually, they learn to weave the tribe's full repertoire of traditional designs from memory, adding new designs which reflect current experiences (e.g., the Afghan-Russian War) or closer contact with other tribes through marriage or assimilation. Eventually, their role in tribal society covers that of both artisan and artist, providing functional artefacts for personal use and trade, while at the same time preserving the tribe's history and religious beliefs. Weaving is the 'high art' in nomadic cultures and, in common with the high art of other cultures, is used to record the tribe's religious, social and cultural beliefs. It is also unique in that it represents the only current example of high art as a totally female preserve.

Tribal weaving is a more all-embracing term than nomadic weaving – it includes not only authentic nomadic items, but also those based on nomadic weaving traditions that are now used by settled tribal people. Tribal kilims may be larger, wider and slightly more sophisticated than nomadic equivalents because settled weavers have greater access to dyes and other materials, as well as the use of fixed vertical looms.

All tribal kilims should be assessed on their overall character and appearance, rather than on their level of technical and compositional perfection. Variations in colouring (*abrashes*) are common, particularly on extended monochrome sections, and there is sometimes a lack of symmetry in a kilim's overall composition or even its physical shape and individual motifs may be strangely articulated, omitted altogether or even replaced by something entirely different. These eccentricities would be totally unacceptable in more sophisticated workshop items, but in tribal weaving they are tolerable and also frequently add to a kilim's individuality, character and ethnic charm.

Authentic tribal kilims are produced in most traditional weaving countries, but primarily Iran, Afghanistan, Turkey, Morocco and, since the Afghan-Russian War, Pakistan. A number of older tribal kilims from the former Soviet Republics in the Caucasus and Central Asia can still be found in the West and contemporary tribal items continue to be produced, although there are not, as yet, sufficiently reliable import/export arrangements in place to ensure a regular supply.

Regional kilims (pls 1, 8, 21, etc.) Produced mainly in the larger villages and towns by people who, regardless of their ethnic origins, weave items that conform to a distinctive localized standard of quality and appearance. The prime criterion for categorizing regional kilims is where, rather than by whom, they are made. Each clearly defined location represents a separate weaving group provided that their kilims have evolved a unique character and appearance that distinguishes them from those produced in neighbouring villages or by tribal weavers in the same area. Regional kilims are no less authentic than kilims of specific tribal origin and some of the 19th- and early 20th-century regional kilims – especially from the Caucasus and Iran – are considered to be among the finest ever produced.

A number of regional weaving groups have a close affinity (both ethnically and stylistically) with specific tribal groups; others produce kilims that are more in keeping with the style, quality and appearance of traditional workshop items; and there are a number in between these two extremes. For example, the and sophistication normally associated with workshop items.

Assessing regional kilims therefore requires the application of different standards, depending on the character of the items produced by each weaving group. Essentially tribal ones (e.g., Van, Shiraz, Bergama) should be judged by the same criteria as authentic tribal kilims and those from the more workshop-influenced weaving groups (e.g., Senneh) should be assessed against higher standards of technical perfection and artistic sophistication.

Regional kilims are produced throughout the entire kilim-weaving region, but particularly in Iran, Turkey and, to a lesser extent, in Afghanistan and North Africa. Older items, especially Caucasian kilims from the 19th and early 20th centuries, can be identified as belonging to distinctive regional weaving groups, but the vast majority of items produced in the Caucasus (and the former Soviet Central Asian Republics), during the latter half of the 20th century, are of contemporary workshop origin, despite the fact that they employed the same designs and were marketed under traditional names, e.g., Shirvan, Karabagh and Kazakh.

Contemporary workshop kilims (pls 9, 11, 12, etc.) Should not be confused with regional kilims, which have their own localized character and appearance and can be allocated to specific weaving groups. Contemporary workshop kilims, in contrast, are a relatively recent innovation aimed at the Western tourist and furnishing markets. They are made in a number of urban centres (which may or may not also produce more traditional items) and employ a wide range of designs from a number of traditional weaving groups, as well as creating original compositions and colour schemes geared specifically to Western decorative needs. At their best, they are extremely attractive, well made and authentic in appearance, but they can also be shoddy, garish and bear little resemblance to traditional kilims. Assessing contemporary workshop kilims should therefore be based on their individual quality and appearance, on their value for money and general decorative or functional suitability. They are produced mainly in Turkey, Afghanistan, North Africa, the Balkans, China and, until 1991, the former Soviet Caucasian Republics.

Complex evil-eye motif found on a Kazakh kilim

Iranian towns of Ardebil, Veramin and Hamadan produce kilims that have distinctive tribal characteristics, but the local weavers are from different ethnic backgrounds and the appearance and structure of their kilims has no direct connection with their tribal origins or weaving traditions. In contrast, the west Iranian towns of Senneh and Bidjar are predominantly Kurdish and their kilims are closely associated with the Kurdish weaving style and characteristics.

The weaving process is normally conducted in workshops of various sizes and levels of sophistication, using fixed or adjustable vertical looms, and – although most of the actual weaving is undertaken by women – men are also involved, often in a supervisory capacity.

Regional designs have evolved over the centuries as a result of the gradual fusion of a number of diverse weaving traditions (both tribal and workshop) and range from being essentially tribal to emulating the sophisticated floral and heraldic motifs found in classic European and Oriental court or workshop items, produced between the 15th and 19th centuries. Some designs –like those found in old Caucasian kilims – frequently combine an essentially tribal boldness of colour and design with the levels of technical excellence

CHAPTER II

How kilims are made

There are a number of different flatweaving techniques used to produce kilims, but they are all based on the principle of interweaving warp and weft strands to create a flat, pileless surface. Kilim weaving is done in sections – the weaver moves vertically and horizontally across the kilim until each segment of the design has been completed – and the design is created by a combination of the colours of the individual warp and weft strands; the insertion of supplementary warps, wefts or pile; and the specific weaving technique.

Warps and wefts

Warps and wefts are the basic constituents of all textiles and in kilims they constitute both the physical structure and the underlying design, which may be further enhanced by the addition of supplementary material. The same material is frequently chosen for both the warp and the weft, but it is not uncommon for different materials to be used – for example, cotton warps in conjunction with woollen wefts.

Warps are the strands of yarn running lengthways (from top to bottom) along the kilim, culminating in the fringes at either end. Warps sometimes help to define the design, but are more often used solely as part of the kilim's physical structure.

Wefts are the strands of yarn that run widthways (from side to side), culminating in the selvedges. The individual colours of the wefts

normally determine the basic composition, as well as forming part of the physical structure of the kilim. Supplementary wefts are also often used to broaden or elaborate the design.

Selvedges and fringes

Selvedges are the sides (or outer edges) of a kilim formed by wrapping the weft strands around the last few warp strands in order to bind the kilim tightly across its width. They are often reinforced by stitching and are more or less the same on all flatwoven or pile rugs.

Fringes are extensions of the warp strands, which protrude lengthways beyond the main body of a kilim, and may be secured in a variety of ways to hold them firmly at the top and bottom edges.

Tied or knotted fringes Formed by tying two or more warp strands into a knot which presses tightly against the final weft strand and then repeating the process across the width of the rug. They are the commonest method of producing fringes and are especially characteristic of Turkish and Kurdish kilims.

Net fringes Tied fringes continued in an interlocking net formation to add an extra touch of artistry to the finished kilim – used by a number of weaving groups.

Simple or kilim fringes Formed by continuing to weave the warp and weft strands beyond the design and then cutting the kilim off the loom. Normally only done on items woven using

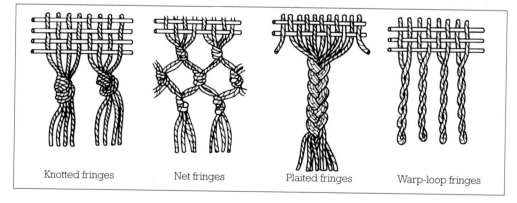

Knotted fringes   Net fringes   Plaited fringes   Warp-loop fringes

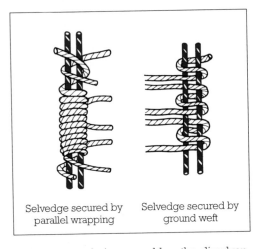

Selvedge secured by
parallel wrapping

Selvedge secured by
ground weft

interlocking warps running widthways along
the end of the kilim.

Plaited fringes Formed by taking three groups
of warp strands (each usually containing three
or four individual strands) and then interweaving them together in exactly the same way that
hair is plaited.

Diagonally plaited fringes Normally only used
with cotton warps and produced by bending
each warp strand back, and then diagonally
interweaving it between five or six adjacent
warp strands, until it presses against the final
weft strand. This is similar to twill or plainweaving, but uses only warp (rather than warp and
weft) strands.

Warp-loop fringes Can only be produced if at
the start of the weaving process the warp
strands are passed over a bar at one end of the
loom to form a continuous loop. The bar is then
removed, leaving the warp strands uncut, naturally securing the last weft strands in place
and allowing them to be tied or plaited for
additional strength. Loop fringes can only be
formed at one end of the kilim, so the opposite
end must be secured by another method.

plainweave techniques and has the disadvantage that the ends eventually unravel unless
they are turned back and sewn.

Loop or chain fringes Made by looping
each individual warp strand over the adjacent
warp strand, then under the next before
finally taking it back in the opposite direction.
This effectively forms a continuous chain of

Weaving techniques

How weaving techniques affect designs

Kilims – unlike pile rugs, which use one
weaving technique for the rug's structure and
another for its design – employ the same technique for both. This means that the method
used to ensure the kilim's physical integrity
also dictates the nature of its design and some
designs can only be achieved when specific
techniques are used.

***Simple monochrome, or speckled composi-
tions, or designs based on horizontal bands***
(pls 5, 17, 26, etc.) Usually obtained by basic
plainweaving techniques, which naturally
secure the kilim across its width. A more complex composition can be created with the
addition of other techniques.

Vertical or diagonal designs (pls 2, 28, 34,
etc.) Break the interlocking pattern and so the
kilim needs to be held in place using another
method, otherwise it will separate along the
edges of each design segment. This is usually
achieved by employing a warp-sharing technique, which is found in a number of variations
throughout the entire kilim-weaving area.

Curvilinear designs (pls 10, 35, etc.) Require
the use of a supplementary weaving technique

(usually weft wrapping or weft insertion) in
conjunction with a basic (normally slitweave or
plainweave) technique.

Plainweave

The simplest and most basic form of flatweaving in which a single weft strand is taken, from
side to side, over and under successive warp
strands. This is repeated in successive rows up
the length of the kilim, in the same manner as
weaving cloth. Plainweaving is used primarily
to produce monochrome areas, which may
cover the entire kilim or be used in conjunction
with another technique to create a more complex design. More complex variations are:

Balanced plainweave Uses warps and wefts of
the same thickness, which means that both
show equally and the design possibilities are
limited to monochrome or (if different-
coloured yarns are used) speckled or tweed
effects. This method does not mix easily with
other techniques and is normally used on the
reverse side of bags, undecorated sections of
semi-pile items and end panels.

Weft-faced plainweave Employs more weft
than warp strands, so that the warp strands are

hidden from view and the kilim's colour scheme and design are restricted to what can be created by the wefts alone – usually either rectangular monochrome sections or different-coloured horizontal bands. This technique is used extensively in North Africa, Afghanistan and parts of Central Asia – both for standard kilims and 'combination' items which employ alternating horizontal strips of kilim and pile.

Warp-faced plainweave The exact opposite of weft-faced plainweave in that it employs more warps than wefts and the colour scheme and design are determined by the colours of the individual warp strands. It shares similar design limitations, but allows for vertical (rather than horizontal) bands.

Twill A variation of plainweave, which involves weaving two (or more) weft strands over two (or more) warp strands in staggered horizontal rows. This produces a zigzag or herring-bone effect. Twill requires a slightly more complex loom, may be either warp-faced or weft-faced and is sometimes used on bags, tent bands and kilim end panels.

Stripweave

A general term for the method of producing kilims by sewing together several strips or segments woven using a variety of techniques. (*See* Jajims and *ghudjeri*, p. 33)

Slitweave

The most basic form of warp sharing which produces reversible kilims and enables relatively complex (mainly diagonal, vertical and crenellated) designs to be woven while simultaneously securing the kilim across its width. This technique requires the weaver to locate a common warp strand – at the junction between two adjacent segments of the design – and then interweave an appropriately coloured weft strand through the intervening warp strands, then wrap it around the common warp strand, and then interweave it back, through the same intervening warps, to its original starting-point. The weaver continues, moving diagonally up the length of the kilim, using successive rows of the same coloured wefts until an entire block of colour (which corresponds to a particular segment of the design) has been produced. The whole process is then repeated for the adjacent design segment, using different-coloured wefts which are in turn wrapped around the same common warp

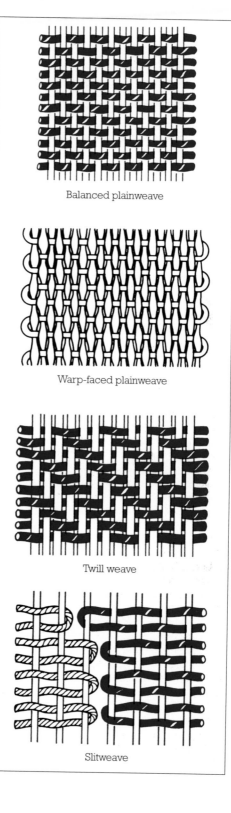

Balanced plainweave

Warp-faced plainweave

Twill weave

Slitweave

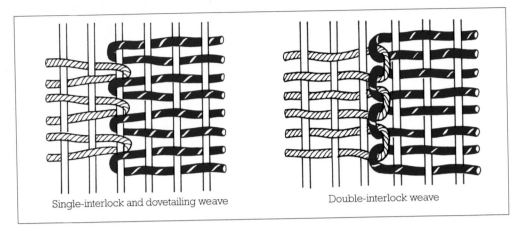

Single-interlock and dovetailing weave

Double-interlock weave

strands. Eventually, all the various coloured segments of the design will be interlocked across common warps and, although there are often some unsecured vertical sections (resulting in the small slits from which the technique gets its name), a sufficient number of common warps are shared to stop the kilim from pulling apart across its width. Slitweaving is ideal for producing diagonal, geometric patterns (e.g., diamonds, triangles, lozenges, stepped crenellations), but inadequate for curvilinear designs. Dealers and collectors once considered it to be the main criterion for defining a kilim and, even though this attitude has changed over the last few decades, it is still the most popular and universal of all flatweaving techniques and is practised by almost every weaving group, except the Berbers in North Africa.

Single-interlock and dovetailing weave Almost identical to slitweaving, except that all the end wefts from an adjacent design segment share the same common warp, allowing vertical patterns to be woven. However, this often results in a slight blurring at the junction between adjacent design segments. The method is referred to as dovetailing if the wefts from adjacent design segments interlock over a common warp on a consistent 1:1 ratio and as single-interlock if the ratio is 1:2 (or more) which produces a more jagged effect. Both are fairly widely used except in Anatolia and North Africa.

Double-interlock weave Works on the same basic principle as single-interlock, but instead of wrapping two different-coloured wefts around a common warp, they are interlocked around each other to form a kind of counter-tension knot. This method also allows vertical patterns to be produced, has the added advantage of providing clear delineation between adjacent segments of the design and does not undermine the strength or tightness of the weave. It is most commonly found on Luri, Bakhtiari and Turkoman kilims, but is sometimes produced by other weaving groups.

Weft-faced patterning

Employs coloured wefts that are woven across the entire width of the kilim, but only show on the front when they are needed to delineate the design. This is achieved by allowing sections of the weft that are not part of the design to float along the back of the kilim, so that they are effectively hidden from view. This technique is often used for producing narrow, horizontal bands of intricate, tightly woven patterns and is employed extensively by the Belouch and other, mainly tribal, weaving groups in Afghanistan, north-east Iran, Central Asia and North Africa.

Warp-faced patterning

Based on the same principle as weft-faced patterning, but reverses the process, so that the warps (rather than the wefts) float along the back of the kilim when not required by the design. However, in warp-faced patterning the tension in the warp strands is lost once anything wider than a few inches has been woven. It is therefore normally confined to the production of tent bands and binding strips, although narrow decorative bands may be stitched together to form a kilim. (*See* Stripweave, p. 21, and *jajims* and *ghudjeri*, p. 33)

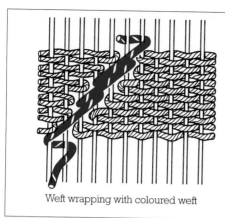

Weft wrapping with coloured weft

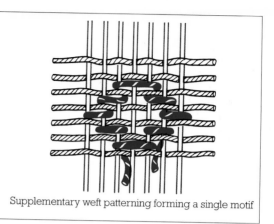

Supplementary weft patterning forming a single motif

Supplementary weft wrapping

A general term for the technique of interweaving additional wefts into a basic weave (e.g., plainweave, slitweave) in order to enhance the design. These additional wefts, which may be of any colour or length, are interwoven during the basic weaving and can be 'wrapped' in a variety of ways to produce a wide range of different motifs and designs. This technique may give a slightly 'sculptured' or 'incised' look to the front of the kilim and may leave short strands of weft material hanging from the back. The main variations are plain and compound weft wrapping and *soumak*:

Plain weft wrapping Does not employ extra wefts, but wraps the existing weft strands over and under the warps (in a ratio of 2:1), building individual blocks of colour and securing the structure by warp sharing. It is rarely used.

Compound weft wrapping Like pile rug weaving in that it interweaves two separate weft strands around the same warp – one provides the colour for the design (in the same way as the knot in pile rug weaving) and the other acts as a ground (or binding) weft, which is used to hold the coloured (design) weft firmly in place. The design weft may be wrapped horizontally, vertically or diagonally depending on the requirements of the composition and may be further elaborated by wrapping over differing numbers of warps. Variations of this technique are used throughout most of the kilim-producing areas.

Soumak A sophisticated weft-wrapping technique, believed to have derived its name from the old Caucasian town of Shemakha. This method produces heavy, durable and often extremely delicately articulated kilims. The term 'Soumak' is often used as a generic name for kilims woven using this technique if their exact origins are unknown.

Brocading A general term that is frequently applied to any supplementary wrapping or insertion technique.

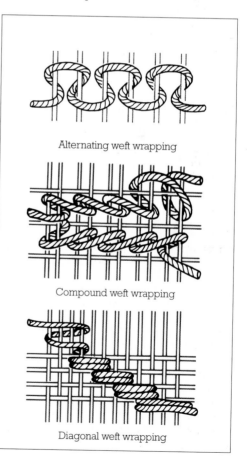

Alternating weft wrapping

Compound weft wrapping

Diagonal weft wrapping

Zilli A weft-wrapping technique, used primarily in Turkey, that gives a distinctive cording or contoured look to the front of the kilim (running parallel to the warps). Sometimes employed as a generic name for unattributed items woven using this technique.

Weft inserts

Frequently used to rectify any loss in the angular symmetry of the weave – caused by variations in the thickness or uneven beating down of the weft stands – through simply inserting additional wefts into the 'lower' side of the kilim until the weft is once more at right angles to the warp. It can also be used to shape the design.

Curved weft inserts Used to create curvilinear designs by deliberately inserting additional wefts until a curve is produced in the line of wefts forming individual motifs; thus enabling the weaver to produce more flowing, naturalistic compositions. It is used by a number of weaving groups, especially in Iran, the Caucasus and parts of Turkey.

Cicim This technique is closely related to weft insertion and weft wrapping and is used to incorporate small, decorative elements into a basic kilim background by wrapping extra wefts continuously around a number of warp strands during the basic weaving process in such a way as to form a distinctive pattern – usually in the form of narrow, semi-linear contours – on the face of the kilim. *Cicim* weaving is generally associated with Turkish kilims, but may also be found in items from Iran and Afghanistan. The term is also sometimes used as a generic name for unattributed items woven using this technique.

Supplementary pile weaving

Used by a number of groups – mainly nomadic and tribal. It normally takes the form of either alternating bands of kilim and pile running throughout the entire length of the item (pl 26) or of a basic kilim structure which has parts of the design highlighted by segments of pile (pl 10). Pile weaving is achieved by tying a short length of yarn around two or more adjacent warp strands so that the ends protrude upwards through a flatwoven foundation to form a pile surface on the front of the kilim. This process is called 'knotting' because when the weft strands have been beaten together to hold the yarn firmly in place a securely tied knot is formed. Each knot creates two individual

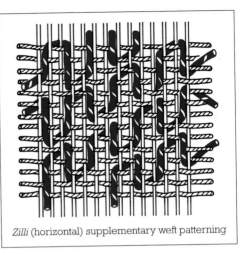

Zilli (horizontal) supplementary weft patterning

strands of pile and the design is created by the juxtaposition of different-coloured pile yarns. Two main types of knot – the Senneh (or Persian) and the Ghiordes (or Turkish) – are used throughout the weaving region, but, apart from being tied slightly differently, both work in essentially the same way and neither is fundamentally superior to the other.

The fineness of the knotting is a reference to the number of individual knots that have been tied to form the pile and is usually measured in either knots per square inch (in^2) or per square metre (m^2). Many dealers use this as the main criterion for assessing the quality of pile rugs, i.e., the greater the number knots, the better the rug. However, the fineness of the knotting is only important according to whether or not it is fine enough to articulate the design to complete satisfaction.

Weft twining

Sometimes used as additional ornamentation on kilims, bags and other woven artefacts. This technique requires the twisting (or twining) of two pairs of different-coloured weft strands around a single warp strand, either clockwise or anti-clockwise, to produce a barber-pole or herring-bone effect. This technique can also be used to produce straps and handles for a variety of bags. (*See* Bags, p. 32)

Tablet or card weaving

Based on a similar principle to weft twining, but is a more complex and intricate technique that uses a piece of stiff card (or leather) to interlock the weft and warp strands.

Looms

Looms differ considerably in size and sophistication, but are all basically a secure frame on which the warp strands are tied. They may be made of wood or metal or a combination of both and be either of fixed dimensions or adjustable so that their inner dimensions can be changed. The type of loom used restricts the size, shape and, to a lesser degree, the sophistication of the kilims that can be produced. In practice, two main types of loom are used in the production of kilims: the horizontal (or nomadic) and the vertical (or village).

Horizontal or nomadic looms

The most simple and primitive looms in contemporary use – they have hardly changed since their inception several millennia ago. They vary slightly in construction, but are all made on the basis of laying out four wooden beams to form a rectangle and then securing them with pegs driven into the ground. This method of weaving is highly compatible with the nomadic lifestyle as it allows unfinished items to be left attached to an opposite pair of beams, rolled into bundles and then strapped on to the back of a horse or camel for transportation to the next encampment. However, it places physical constraints on the weaver, who is unable to reach more than about half a metre (a couple of feet) across the kilim from any side. This makes it difficult to produce large items or ones more than about one metre (3' to 4') wide and strains the weaver's ability to articulate extremely intricate designs. Consequently, most nomadic kilims are usually either fairly small or long and narrow. (*See* Tribal kilims, p. 16)

Vertical looms

Permanent structures, with either fixed or adjustable inner dimensions, used by settled weavers from village, regional and contemporary workshop groups. The main advantage of vertical looms is that they allow the weaver unrestricted access across the entire width of the kilim, facilitating the creation of intricate designs and the production of items whose width is only restricted by that of the inner widthways dimensions of the loom.

Village looms Have fixed dimensions and consequently restrict the size of the items that can be woven to less than the height and width of the loom. However, they still provide the weaver with easy access across the kilim's entire width. Village looms are used extensively by semi-nomadic and settled tribal weavers, and also by some regional weaving groups.

Semi-portable vertical looms Occasionally used by nomadic weavers, during periods of extended encampment, but many rely exclusively on traditional horizontal looms.

Adjustable looms Normally of fixed dimensions across their width, but one of their two horizontal beams on which the warps are tied (usually the lower) is made in such a way that allows it to be adjustable. The two most common examples of adjustable looms are the Tabriz loom, which has a retractable beam capable of shifting the completed section of the kilim to the rear of the loom, and the roller loom, which replaces the bottom horizontal beam with a roller mechanism that allows the finished portion of the kilim to be rolled around a cylinder. Both effectively extend the vertical weaving dimensions, allowing the weaving of

Vertical village loom

Horizontal or nomadic loom

the same height throughout the entire weaving process, which makes it quicker and easier for them to articulate the design. Adjustable looms are used extensively in contemporary workshop weaving.

items considerably longer than the height of the loom. They also enable the weavers to sit at

Tools

The beating comb Used to press (or beat) the weft strands into place, pushing each new row tightly against the previous row to ensure the compactness of the finished kilim. Beating combs are basically larger, tougher versions of ordinary hair combs and may be made of metal or wood or a combination of both. Individual weavers may have several versions that vary slightly in size and construction, but they all have the same basic function.

The shuttle Basically a stick, with notches cut into the ends to hold the weft threads, that is passed over and under the warp strands in order to weave the kilim. Weavers often prefer to weave entirely by hand and only use the shuttle in exceptional circumstances or on certain areas of a kilim where shuttle weaving is quicker and easier. The use of a shuttle makes no difference to a kilim's handwoven authenticity and value.

The knife or scissors Used to cut and trim the warp and weft strands. The knife may have a slightly curved blade to help unpick any imperfectly woven strands.

Materials

All kilims are normally made only with natural fibres and any item containing large amounts of synthetic material will almost certainly have been machine made. However, some tribal kilims (particularly those produced by nomads) may be decorated with strands of brightly coloured synthetic fibres, glass beads, pieces of gold or silver foil and an assortment of other found material.

Wool

The most commonly used, most suitable and most versatile kilim-making material – it is pliable, durable, easy to work and also contains lanolin and other natural oils, which help the kilim to retain its suppleness, resist dirt and make it easy to clean. Wool is frequently the only material used – i.e., for both warps and wefts. It may also be employed in conjunction with other materials, e.g., as the weft on items with cotton warps or as the warp and weft on kilims with silk supplementary patterning.

There are several different types of wool, some more suitable for kilim-making than others, and good kilim wool needs to combine suppleness with durability and tensile strength with the capacity to be spun easily into yarns. It is derived from varieties of sheep – both wild and domesticated – common to a number of parts of the kilim-weaving region, each producing wool of slightly different character and quality.

The quality of wool from any breed of sheep is largely determined by local grazing and climate, and sheep reared in the lusher, more commodious grazing lands normally produce softer, more lustrous wool than those reared in the hot, desert regions. However, as a general rule, the wool used for kilim-making is of good quality and, provided a kilim is treated correctly, should last for many years.

Cotton

Employed primarily for warps and to provide highlights – usually white – in a design. It is also sometimes used for supplementary wefts, normally in conjunction with standard woollen wefts. However, some purely cotton flatweaves are produced, mainly in Afghanistan, Turkey and India (see *Sutrangis* and *dhurries*, p. 33). Cotton is not as versatile or suitable a kilim-weaving material as wool, but it does have some advantages: it is stronger, more vermin resistant, keeps its shape better, can be spun into thinner strands and is in plentiful supply – growing wild in many parts of the weaving region. It is, however, susceptible to mildew, so kilims with cotton foundations should not be placed on the floor near pots that contain houseplants.

Mercerized cotton Known in the trade as 'art' (or 'artificial') silk. Some 'art' silk kilims are very occasionally produced (mainly by contemporary workshops).

Silk

Derived from a species of moth (*bombix mori*) commonly known as the silkworm, which is native to Iran, China and other parts of the weaving region. Two kinds of silk are used in weaving: raw silk, also known as 'drawn' or 'reeled' silk because it is drawn or reeled directly from the cocoon, and waste silk, which is derived from damaged cocoons and has to be carded and spun like wool or cotton. It is also much cheaper than drawn silk and is the type most often used in kilim weaving.

Silk is extremely strong and durable and can be spun into the very thin strands needed for exceptionally fine patterning. It has a natural iridescence that can enhance any design and is believed to repel malevolent psychic forces – silk garments traditionally protect the wearer from spells. It is more expensive than wool or cotton, scuffs easily, retains creases (silk items should always be rolled, never folded) and melts if it comes into contact with a flame or excessive heat, making it necessary to treat silk kilims with extra care. A number of silk kilims were woven in Iran, Turkey, Central Asia and some other parts of the weaving area up until the late 19th century, but very few are now produced. However, silk is still used for supplementary patterning by a number of contemporary weaving groups, including tribal and nomadic. For 'art' silk *see* Mercerized cotton.

Additional materials

Hair Derived from goats, camels and horses is also used – normally with wool – by some nomadic and tribal weaving groups. Goat hair has a silky sheen, which, when mixed with wool, can enhance the patina and appearance of the kilim; it is sometimes used as warp or selvedge binding material because of its durability and tensile strength. Camel hair is also extremely strong and durable and is a better insulator than wool. It may be used to reinforce or strengthen a predominantly woollen kilim. Horse hair, taken from the mane and tail, is employed by a number of nomadic groups to decorate tassels and fringes, especially in Central Asia.

Decorative found materials Metal threads (usually gold and silver), synthetic fibres (brightly coloured rayon, nylon, etc.), beads, shells, coins, pieces of coloured metal (e.g., from tin cans) and almost any small, brightly coloured object that captures the weaver's interest may be used on a wide range of nomadic and tribal kilims.

The preparation of materials

Only wool requires shearing, but the other four stages apply to all fibrous kilim-making materials.

Shearing Undertaken once or sometimes twice a year – normally in the spring and perhaps the late summer or early autumn. It is usually done by hand, although electric shearing may be used in the larger commercial shearing centres. The wool is then cleaned, usually by repeated washing in clean water and carefully dried between each wash. However, some weaving groups have their own distinctive methods of cleaning. For instance, the Qashga'i, of southern Iran, scour the wool with boiling water and bicarbonate of soda; and in some parts of the Caucasus the dirt is beaten out with thin boards or flat stones. However, regardless of the washing process, the dry wool is then sent for carding.

Washing Normally undertaken shortly after the yarn has been cleaned, usually by rinsing it in a weak solution of soda and soap, in preparation for carding, spinning and dyeing.

Carding The process that teases the wool into longer, straighter fibres by repeatedly drawing them through the carder's fingers or over and through a series of pins inserted into a block of wood, which disentangles the fibres so that they are straight enough to be spun into yarn.

Spinning Teasing or stretching the fibres, either by hand or machine, into continuous strands is necessary to form a yarn capable of being woven. The strands are then secured by being twisted in opposite directions to each other – either clockwise (known as a 'Z' twist) or anti-clockwise (known as an 'S' twist). Hand-spun yarn is common among tribal weavers, but machine-spun yarn is generally used by contemporary workshop and most regional weaving groups.

Note Ply is the term used to describe the individual strands that make up the yarn. If a length of yarn contains three strands it is referred to as 3-ply (five strands 5-ply, etc.) and, as a general rule, the more plies in the yarn, the thicker and stronger it will be.

Dyeing and colours

The dyeing process is a vitally important part of kilim-making because if the dyes are fugitive (i.e., their colour changes) or the wrong shade, the entire kilim may be ruined. Kilim dealers and producers are also aware that people buy kilims as much for their colour schemes as for their designs. Considerable care is therefore taken, both in choosing and preparing the dyes and also in executing the dyeing process. This is usually composed of three stages and the yarn is left to dry between each.

Mordanting A process that helps bond the dye to the fibres by the use of a chemical (or mordant). This normally takes place prior to dyeing and involves soaking the yarn for about an hour in a mordant bath – usually a weak solution of either alum, copper sulphate, chrome, copperas (ferrous sulphate), tin or uric acid (urine). Alternatively, the mordant solution is simply added to the dye or, occasionally, the yarn is mordanted afterwards.

Dyeing The yarn is soaked in a bath of appropriately coloured dye until the correct intensity of tone has been obtained. Dyeing is very much a male preserve – in tribal cultures the dyer is often considered to be a tribal wise man whose counsel may be sought on a wide variety of matters – and is regarded as a science whose secrets are jealously guarded and handed down from generation to generation.

Washing The final process, undertaken once the weaving has been completed, that is necessary to remove surface dirt and excess dye and also to give the kilim its characteristic finish. Some items are simply washed in soap and water, but others may be soaked (or washed) in a chemical solution, which usually includes some form of moth-proofing. However, the main purpose of a chemical wash is usually to mellow or tone down the colours artificially, making them more compatible with Western decorative tastes and frequently reproducing the effects of age.

Natural or vegetable dyes

Derived from a number of vegetable, animal and mineral sources, which frequently originated locally, although they are now often imported from other areas. Some natural pigments are intrinsically fugitive and were only used in the past because they were the best available, but many produce a quality of colour and tone – especially as they begin to mellow with age – that is far superior to that of even the best chemical alternatives around today. However, there are some colours (e.g., greens and purples) for which there are very few suitable natural sources and the dyer has to combine two or more pigments in order to produce the required colour or tone. This cannot always be successfully repeated. Some natural dyes are also expensive or difficult to obtain and even ones that are cheap and plentiful, such as indigo, may have the inherent problem of not necessarily producing the exact same shade of colour because of the differing amounts of pigment in each plant. Many collectors cherish these variations in tone as being an integral part of a kilim's individuality and ethnic charm. However, department stores and other major retail outlets often require a standard of quality control that does not allow for any individual tonal variations.

Natural dyes are still used extensively by tribal weavers, either on their own or in combination with synthetic dyes. Generally most tribal (and a number of regional) weavers will have used natural dyes for most of their basic colours – reds, blues, etc. – with perhaps synthetic dyes for some of the supplementary shades.

Blue Derived almost exclusively from plants of the ubiquitous *Indigofera* and *Isatis tinctoria* (woad) genera, referred to collectively as indigo, which apart from producing a wide variety of beautiful and stable shades, also help to preserve the yarn. This may be because indigo is one of the very few pigments that is colourfast without the addition of an abrasive mordant (which can slightly undermine natural fibres).

Red Usually obtained either from the indigenous madder plant (*Rubia tinctorum*) or, to a lesser degree, from other plant sources, including poppy and tulip petals, rhubarb and rose roots, cherry skins and the bark of the jujube tree. Certain shades may be obtained from the crushed bodies of the female cochineal insect (*Dactylopius coccus*) or from two other insects – kermes (*Chermes abietis*) and lac (*Laccifer lacca*).

Yellow Derived from several plant species, containing one or more pigments (e.g., quercetin, apigenin, fisetin, crocin and datiscetin), capable of producing a variety of yellow and yellowish orange shades. Quercetin is found in St John's wort, onion, spurge, buckthorn, dyer's camomile and tanner's sumach and produces a standard yellow or yellowish brown. Apigenin is contained in camomile, wild camomile and dyer's weed and produces a bright to standard yellow. Datiscetin, found in bastard hemp, gives a brilliant yellow – especially when combined with an alum mordant. Fisetin and crocin, in dyer's sumach and the saffron crocus respectively, both produce a yellowish orange. A number of other plants – centaury, turmeric, artemisia, vine leaves, rhubarb, *Sophora japonica*, *Gardenia jasminoides* and varieties of the reseda plant – may also be used.

Orange Normally produced by combining red and yellow pigments, but henna, grass roots, plum bark and some of the plants containing yellowish orange pigments may also be used.

Black Made from plants with a high tannin content, such as pomegranate peel, oak apples, knobbly oak and tanner's sumach (*see* Yellow). They are often combined with iron rust or filings, which unfortunately tend to eventually corrode (disintegrate) the yarn.

Tan and brown Made from acorn cups and walnut husks, but natural brown wool is often preferred.

Purple and violet Normally produced by mixing red and blue pigments, but grape skins and reddish blue pigments (such as cochineal) may also be used.

Additional colours and shades Derived from a wide range of flowers, leaves, barks, nutshells, berries, insects, minerals and earth.

Synthetic dyes

Found in most contemporary workshop kilims and, to a lesser degree, in regional and tribal items – especially used for colours or tones that are difficult to obtain using natural dyes. The first synthetic 'aniline' dye was a violet colorant called fuchsine, which an English chemist derived from benzene in 1856. It was followed, three years later, by the development of a similar dye called mauveine in France. After these discoveries additional colorants were rapidly developed. They revolutionized the commercial production of textiles by providing an almost limitless supply of cheap and readily available dyestuff and became a plentiful source of new colours for rug and kilim weavers. Unfortunately, many of these early aniline dyes were often both fugitive and unattractive, and were later banned in several weaving countries – especially in Iran, where a dyer found using aniline dyes risked having his right arm amputated and his dyehouse burnt to the ground. However, the discovery of much more stable and attractive chrome dyes, between the First and Second World Wars, changed the attitude towards synthetic dyes. Now they are in common usage and are generally of excellent quality, although they perhaps lack the subtlety of some natural pigments, especially as they mellow with age. Today's buyers can be sure that the colours in their kilim, whether synthetic or natural, will remain stable or improve slightly with age.

Terms and expressions

Fugitive Describes pigments whose colours are unstable after relatively short-term exposure to light.

Abrash Term used to describe a change in the tone or intensity of an individual colour that does not correspond to a new element in the design. An *abrash* usually takes the form of either a sudden lightening or darkening of a specific colour in a continuous monochrome area (pl 28) or a similar variation in the tone of the same colour used in different parts of the kilim (pl 16). This is normally the result of changing to a new batch of separately dyed yarn part way through the weaving process – both batches may look the same when new, but the colours may fade at different rates.

Abrashes are common and perfectly acceptable in tribal kilims and tribal-influenced regional items. A number of dealers and collectors believe that *abrashes* – provided they are not too severe – may even add to a kilim's character and appearance, giving it an extra degree of individuality and ethnic charm. They are less acceptable in contemporary workshop kilims and workshop-influenced regional items; although some are now specifically made to echo older, more tribal kilims and may contain a deliberate *abrash*.

Mellowness Term used to describe the natural process of fading that takes place when pigments (especially those found in natural dyes) are exposed to light. It can take several years for colours to lose their intensity and soften to what is generally considered to be the aesthetically optimum mellowness of tone. Consequently, a number of weaving groups have traditionally produced kilims with extremely bright and, sometimes deliberately, garish colours and have relied on the natural effects of sunlight to mellow and harmonize the pigments. Eventually this produces the optimum colour scheme, ten or twenty years after the kilim has been taken off the loom.

Chemical washes may now be used to create an immediate tonal mellowness, rather than waiting several years for it to happen naturally. This practice is especially common with contemporary workshop items that are designed to either emulate tribal kilims or copy the items produced by older, sometimes no longer active, weaving groups.

The relationship between colour and age

Colours fade as a result of prolonged exposure to sunlight, so there is a general assumption that the more the colours have faded or mellowed the older the kilim must be. This is essentially true, but also the stronger the light, the more quickly the colours will fade.

Chemical washes can also emulate the effects of ageing and one has to be extremely careful about jumping to the conclusion that just because the colours have faded the kilim must therefore be old. (*See* Washing, p. 28)

The meaning of individual colours

This varies considerably from culture to culture, but generally is not as symbolically important in the predominately Islamic kilim-producing countries as it is in China, Tibet and the other mainly Buddhist-Taoist countries of the Far East. The meaning and symbolism of colours is generally secondary to that of motifs and designs and among many weaving groups has little or no significance whatsoever.

Green (the colour of Mohammed's coat) is, however, considered sacred in most Muslim countries and is rarely used as a predominant colour. Red is widely believed to be the colour of wealth, prosperity and rejoicing. Orange is generally synonymous with piety and devotion. Blue symbolizes heaven (and consequently peace and serenity) in Iran; and power and authority among some of the Mongol-Turkic tribesmen of Central Asia. White is associated with grief by the Persians, Indians and Chinese.

Shapes and sizes

Kilims are made in a number of relatively standard shapes and sizes that correspond to their function, either as independent items or as part of a traditional floor arrangement (*see* p. 36). Many of which are known by specific names. *Ceyrik*: Turkish name for kilims about 4' 6" x 2' 9" (1.37 x 0.84 m). *Dozar* (pl 15, etc.):

Persian name meaning two *zars* (a *zar* is a unit of measurement, about 4' 2" or 1.28 m) applied to items around 8' long (two *zars*) and 5–6' wide (2.44 x 1.52–1.83 m). *Kellegi* (pl 2, etc.): derived from the Persian word *kelley* (meaning 'head') and applied to the head or top kilim in the traditional floor arrangement (pl 2). It can measure anything from 12–24' long x 6–8' wide (3.66–7.32 x 1.83–2.44 m). *Kenareh* (pl 6, etc.): from the Persian word *kenar* (meaning 'side') and is a slightly smaller and narrower version of a *kellegi* used at the side in the traditional floor arrangement. *Khali* or *qali* (pl 18, etc.): Turkoman and Persian terms that literally mean 'carpet' and can be applied to any large, room-sized items of 10' x 6' (3.05 x 1.83 m) or even larger. *Pushti* or *yastik*: Persian and Turkish words for small bedside items of around 3' x 2' (0.91 x 0.61 m). *Yastik* also means cushion. *Sarai kilem*: Kirghiz name for a palace, or a very large carpet, or kilim. *Seccade* (pl 35, etc.): Turkish name for items of around 6' 6" x 3' 9" (1.98 x 1.14 m). *Zaronim* (pl 34, etc.): Persian name, meaning a *zar* and a half (*see dozar*), applied to items about 6' x 4' (1.83 x 1.22 m) or 5' x 3' 6" (1.52 x 1.07 m).

Special kilims, bags and artefacts

In addition to standard kilims, a wide range of items are produced – mainly by nomadic and other tribal weavers – that have a special purpose or function. These include eating cloths, door flaps, prayer rugs, blankets, bags, animal trappings and other woven artefacts, which are frequently marketed under the name of their function. However, items with the same basic function may be known by a different name in each weaving region, for instance, a small kit bag is called a *chavadan* by the Kirghiz and a *torbah* in other parts of Central Asia.

It is not, as yet, common practice among dealers to apply universal names, which can be confusing for the collector who may be unsure whether a bag marketed as a *chanteh*, for example, is different to one referred to as a *kap* or if they are simply different local names for the same item. Many dealers use a generic (or collective) name for certain items, regardless of their origin or local name and it is now fairly common for small bags of uncertain origin or usage to be marketed as *torbahs*, and larger ones as *juvals*. However, these names are not applied consistently. Dealers sometimes try to establish a more exact attribution, but this can be extremely difficult because a number of different tribal items are of very similar structure and appearance and, by the time they reach the West, their trail of provenance has often been totally obscured. It is also virtually impossible, without chemical analysis, to tell whether a particular small bag was used to store salt (making it a *namakdan*) or other personal or household goods. However, the structure and appearance of some specialized items is sufficiently distinct to enable identification, although there will always be some items that will defy any attempt to discover their exact origins and the purposes for which they were made.

Kilims for special purposes

Soufrehs or **soufrais** (pl 25) Take their name from the Farsi (Persian) word for cloth and are used for several functions connected with preparing and eating food. For example, *soufreh-i-nan* 'cloth for baking' and *soufreh-i-ghamir* 'cloth for mixing/sieving flour'. Eating cloths are normally referred to simply as *soufrehs* and vary enormously in size – from small, rectangular mats for personal use to extremely long, narrow runners for communal eating. They are woven in several standard techniques, including alternating bands of kilim and pile rug, and produced by a number of nomadic and tribal weavers in Iran, Afghanistan, Central Asia and, to a lesser degree, elsewhere.

Note Dasterkan or *dashterkhan* (pl 19) is an alternative name for an eating cloth, normally applied only to items from the Belouch, Taimani (Aimaq) and other Central Asian tribal weaving groups.

Rukorssi An abbreviated term for *soufreh-i-rukorssi* (cloth to cover the oven). They are generally about one third of a metre square (4' sq) and are used as oven and brazier covers, and sometimes double up as additional blankets in the winter.

Prayer mats or rugs (pl 37) Used specifically to kneel upon when praying and are normally relatively small (about 5' x 3', 13 cm x 8 cm). They may vary in design from simple monochrome fields to elaborate *mihrab* and tree-of-life schemes. Functional prayer mats should not be confused with more general purpose items woven in a prayer-rug design. (*See* Chapter V)

Saphs Prayer mats containing a multiple prayer-rug design – usually of repeating *mihrabs*. They are often referred to as family prayer rugs, although, in practice, most are probably just decorative.

Other special items *Ayatlyk*: Turkoman name for a funerary rug or kilim. *Dezlik*: Turkoman name for a small tent door rug or kilim, which doubles up as a collar for the lead camel in a wedding procession. *Eshik tysh*: Kirghiz name for a door hanging. *Germetch*: Turkoman name for any item designed to fit the threshold of a tent door. *Hatchli* or *enssi*: common terms for tent-door hangings; also the names given to a specific design (*see* p. 100). *Kosh jabyk*: Kirghiz name for a hanging cot or cradle. *Namazlyk*: common name throughout Central Asia for a prayer mat. *Ojakbashi*: Turkoman name for a hearth rug or a kilim. *Purdah*: kilim or other textile used to separate male from female living quarters.

Bags

A wide range of bags are produced by the majority of nomadic weaving groups and, to a lesser extent, by some settled 'tribal' weavers. They are marketed under a number of different names, which may or may not be the ones used by the actual weavers. This may make their original purpose or function extremely difficult to ascertain, but it is generally safe to assume that they are made for personal (or collective) usage and sold or bartered only after replacements have been woven. However, as bags become increasingly popular in the West, it is possible that they may start to be produced specifically for export.

Personal bags (pls 23, 38) Used for carrying personal possessions (tobacco, coins, jewelry, sewing material, etc.). They are produced by most nomadic and a few settled tribal weaving groups. They vary in size and shape, but are generally small enough either to fit into a pocket or to be carried easily with a shoulder-strap and may be single bags (with or without flaps) containing one or more compartments or wallet-like double bags that can be folded over.

Chanteh, canta, chanta and kap (pl 38): common names for these small, general purpose bags. The following are Turkoman names. *Aina khalta*: a small mirror bag. *Chinakap*: a bowl case. *Igsalik*: a spindle bag. *Kese*: a wallet or money bag. *Namakdan* (pl 23): a general name applied to the salt bags, used by herdsmen, which have a distinctive bottle-shaped neck.

Tent bags (pls 20, 24) Used inside the tent to store food, clothes, utensils and other items. They vary in shape and size, and may double up as cushions or kit bags. *Chuval, juval, bashtyk* and *napramach*: common names for general purpose, usually quite large, tent bags. *Jallar* (pl 20): the general name for a large, horizontal bag with a distinctive long fringe along the bottom. It is hung from the tent wall and used for general storage. *Maffrash* (pl 24): the common name given to bedding bags, which are woven by young girls as an essential part of their dowry and used to store bedding, clothes and other personal possessions. They are normally secured by ties, toggles or even metal buckles.

Kit bags Relatively small, rarely more than 1' 6" sq (45 cm sq) and generally used on a day-to-day basis to carry around larger personal items (clothes, tools, food, etc.), but they also double up as tent bags. *Torbah, torba, chavadan, karshin, karchin* and *shabadan* are all common names for these items.

Cushions A number of bags are woven by several nomadic and settled tribal weaving groups for use as cushions or seats and are stuffed with cotton or wools. They vary considerably in size and shape and are frequently employed by settled weavers as permanent items of furniture, although nomads also use them for transporting various items between encampments. These cushions and seats are commonly called *balisht, yastik, tatrayin* and *usada*.

Saddle-bags Most nomadic weavers produce saddle-bags of varying sizes and degrees of sophistication, which are designed to fit the backs of horses, donkeys and camels. They are used both for the transportation of goods and for ceremonial purposes. Saddle-bags may undergo considerable wear and tear before reaching the West and it is not uncommon for only one half of the original double bag to have survived. Also known as *khordin, khurgin, hurgin, heybe* and *keite*.

Artefacts and animal trappings

A wide variety of bridles, harnesses, blankets and other functional and decorative trappings are made for horses, camels and donkeys by most nomadic and some tribal weaving groups. They may be either primarily decorative or functional or both and are becoming increasingly collectable in their own rights.

They range in sophistication from simple monochrome plainweaves to highly elaborate kilim and pile rug combinations that often contain additional ornamentation, such as beads, bells, coins and shells. Each type of artefact has its own regional or tribal name and may be marketed in the West by any one of these or by their corresponding Western terms, i.e., donkey bridal, camel headdress or horse blanket. *Asmalyk*: Turkoman for the twin-flanked trapping used primarily on wedding camels. *Deve baslik*: the Turkish name for a camel's headdress, usually decorated with cowrie shells. *Eyerlik*: Turkoman for a saddle-cloth. (*See* Saddle-bags, p. 32)

Tent bands Long strips of woven material, normally between 2" (5 cm) and 12" (30 cm) wide, used to decorate tents, but also to tie baggage, lash roofing poles and act as tent-securing ropes. *Iolem* and *kapunuk* are common terms.

Tent-pole covers Cylindrical bags used as sleeves to house tent poles during transportation: usually marketed as either *kola-i-chergh, uuk bash, uuk kap* or simply tent-pole bags.

Miscellaneous weavings

There are also a number of items produced in the kilim-weaving region that cannot be categorized as kilims, but are nevertheless closely associated with traditional kilim-weaving and are collectable in their own right.

Dhurries Flatweaves, usually cotton, that were originally produced by prisoners in India, but are now woven extensively in workshops throughout India and, to a lesser extent, Pakistan. They are equivalent to *sutrangis*.

Ikats (pl 42) Flatweaves, waxed on the surface, that are used primarily as wall-hangings or to make coats and other outer clothes. They are normally associated with certain parts of Central Asia (especially Uzbekistan and Afghanistan), where extremely fine waxed-silk examples are made, although Indonesia now produces waxed-cotton *ikats*.

Jajims and ghudjeri (pl 41) Names given to items, produced by sewing together narrow strips of kilim material (normally woven in a warp-faced patterning technique), which are used as, for example, floor-coverings, bedspreads and horse blankets. *Jajims* are woven primarily by tribal groups, particularly in Iran (e.g., Qashga'i, Luri, Khamseh, Shahsavan, Bakhtiari) and *ghudjeri* by various Turkomen and Turkic tribes in Central Asia. (*See* Stripweave, p. 21)

Moj Persian for 'wave', applied to stripwoven blankets, bed-covers and similar items produced – mainly by settled Qashga'i and Luri weavers – in workshops throughout Iran.

Namad General term used for 'felt' (made by soaking wool and then pressing it so that the fibres compact and bind). It is employed, mainly by nomadic and semi-nomadic tribesmen, to make a wide range of items, including rugs, hats, bags, animal trappings, coats, boots and other garments.

Sileh Name applied to a group of old Caucasian rugs, woven in a variation of the *soumak* technique, featuring large 'S'-shaped motifs that are usually interpreted as mythological dragons. Some authorities argue that the dragons are more likely to be stylized snakes or possibly variations of the swastika motif. Their exact place of origin is ascribed by different authorities to Shirvan, Kuba, Daghestan and possibly Karabagh, but it is generally accepted that they were woven somewhere in the Caucasus until the late 19th or early 20th centuries. Contemporary kilims employing this design are now produced in other countries, but these items should not be confused with original Caucasian *silehs*, which are now extremely collectable and expensive.

Sutrangis Cotton flatweaves woven predominantly by the inmates of Maimana prison and other provincial jails in Afghanistan. They are usually composed of simple triangles and diamonds in pastel colours and may range in size from small mats to huge carpets of up to 200 sq ft (or 19 sq m). They are the Afghan equivalent of *dhurries*.

Verneh (pl 39) Originally the name given to a group of old Caucasian kilims produced until the early to mid 20th century (woven using either *soumak* or embroidery techniques and primarily for export). They normally feature rectangular and other geometric forms – frequently decorated inwardly with stylized birds – and have a relatively sombre colour scheme of deep reds, blues and white. Most authorities believe that they were made in the south-eastern Caucasus (Shirvan, Kuba, etc.), but it is possible that this type of weaving was also practised elsewhere. Some contemporary weaving groups (especially the Shahsavan) produce similar items that are frequently marketed as *vernehs*, although they should not be confused with the originals, which are much more collectable and expensive.

CHAPTER III

Buying a kilim

Before buying a kilim always ask yourself 'why you want it' and 'how much you can afford to pay'. No matter how attractive or inexpensive a kilim may be, it can be a waste of money if it does not fit the space allocated, or blend into its chosen surroundings, or fulfil the function for which it was bought. Similarly, there is no point in buying an expensive antique kilim to put on the floor in an area of heavy traffic when a cheaper, contemporary item will not only be perfectly adequate, but will also probably resist the inevitable wear and tear to a much higher degree. Remember that some kilims, which may be excellent value as general furnishing items, are unlikely to prove good long-term investments, whereas others, with a much better investment potential, may be less suited to your immediate decorative needs.

Both kilims and pile rugs generally represent excellent value for money and many medium-priced items are often as cheap, if not cheaper, than decent quality machine-made floor coverings, as well as retaining their resale value to a much higher degree. Both are also normally well made, attractive, durable and possess the character and uniqueness of being handmade.

Kilims are more versatile than pile rugs, however, as they function equally well as floor-coverings, wall-hangings, furniture covers, bags and peripheral decorations. They are also lighter, more manoeuvrable, easier to transport and generally less expensive. They are not usually as hard-wearing, but are still extremely durable, especially those woven in *soumak* or other heavy-duty weaves.

Decorative considerations

Some kilims are collected primarily as investments, but the vast majority are bought by people who simply want something to serve a practical function and enhance the appearance of their homes. The fact that a kilim might hold or increase its value over the years is viewed as a possible bonus, without being the reason why it was initially bought. Consequently, the most important purchasing criteria – in addition to quality – are colour, design, shape, size and general suitability.

Colour

The overall decorative impact of a kilim on a room is normally governed more by its colours than its design, so there is often considerable flexibility in the choice of style and design of a kilim provided its colour scheme is compatible with the surrounding decor. Consequently, special attention needs to be given to finding an item that is tonally suitable for a specific room. Some kilims are produced in pastel or muted colours, but the majority employ deeper, more primary shades that may initially seem to be intrinsically incompatible with

most Western decorative schemes. In practice, however, they often combine surprising well with the generally more pastel tones of Western decor. Consequently, prospective buyers should have little difficulty in finding something suitable provided they are prepared to shop around. Many retail outlets offer some form of home trial and, if in doubt, it is always advisable to take advantage of this facility.

A harmonious effect Created by choosing a kilim that reflects the overall tonality of the room (pastel, rich, sombre, etc.) or ensuring that at least one colour is present in both the room and the kilim. It need not be the dominant colour in either – more effective results are frequently obtained by matching respective subsidiary colours or a subsidiary colour in the room with a dominant one in the kilim (or vice versa). For example, a room with pastel yellows can be harmoniously invigorated by a predominantly red kilim with subsidiary yellow or yellow-ochre elements in the design.

A contrasting effect Achieved by choosing a kilim whose colours provide a striking counterpoint to the colours in the room. Care needs to be taken to ensure that the two sets of colours do not clash or cancel each other out. Contrast often works best in a room that is tonally neutral (e.g., with white or monochrome pastel walls), which will allow the stronger colours in the kilim to create the room's overall colour focus. A more subtle form of contrast can be obtained by introducing a kilim with richer, deeper shades of the room's dominant colour. For example, a pale blue decor can be enlivened by a kilim with strong shades of red and blue.

Pastel shades (pls 11, 14, 34, etc.) Less common in kilims than in pile rugs, but a number of kilims produced are geared specifically towards Western decorative tastes, especially those made by contemporary workshop groups. Some tribal and regional weaving groups also weave items dominated by pale yellow and orange ochres, light browns and white; some older items, in addition, now have beautifully muted (or mellowed) reds and blues. Pastel shades are compatible with most Western decorative schemes – especially in bedrooms – and normally present few problems of tonal suitability, although care should to be taken with their exact placement because they show dirt and scuff marks more easily than deeper shades.

Rich shades (pls 12, 18, etc.) Found in kilims from most weaving regions and easily assimilated into rooms with classic furnishings (e.g., solid, dark-stained wooden furniture and richly patterned fabrics). Smaller items can also work well in lighter, more modern surroundings by providing an opulent focal point, but care needs to be taken with large, room-sized kilims because they may be too dominant, swamping the decorative impact of the other furnishings.

Strong, dark or sombre shades (pls 5, 18, 26, etc.) Common in Belouch and some other (mainly tribal) kilims – especially suited to rooms that have a predominance of natural wood and relatively neutral or autumnal decor such as plain, slightly austere farmhouse, or country cottage settings, or offices, dens and studies.

Vibrant shades (pls 6, 30, 36, etc.) Produced by a number of weaving groups throughout Iran (e.g., Veramin), Turkey (e.g., Manastir) and North Africa (e.g., Gafsa). Vibrant shades can complement and invigorate any type of decor provided there is some mutual colour harmony and care is taken to choose an item that does not overpower the room.

Design

The design of a kilim usually has less impact on the surroundings than its colour – provided the colours are compatible. However, they are vital to the intrinsic attractiveness of a kilim and its ability to enhance or detract from the decorative impact of a room.

Geometric designs (pls 7, 12, 28, etc.) Found in kilims from almost every weaving group throughout the entire weaving region. They can be compatible with almost every type of decor, providing there is some degree of colour harmony, but are perhaps most suited to rooms which have plain, more angular Scandinavian-style furniture and furnishings.

Curvilinear designs (pls 11, 35, 42, etc.) Usually only found in kilims produced by contemporary workshop and some of the more sophisticated regional weaving groups and, even then, there is frequently a geometric edge to the articulation of the motifs. These designs often find their best expression in luxurious or classically furnished surroundings, but can also add a touch of opulence to more plainly furnished rooms.

Repeating designs (pls 4, 9, 31, etc.) Based on a single motif or group of motifs repeated throughout the kilim. The pattern is therefore the same from any angle, allowing considerable scope in the way a kilim can be placed – vital with runners and room-sized items.

Centralized designs (pls 21, 29, 34, etc.) Employ a single centralized motif or group of motifs (frequently a medallion). This type of design is produced by several weaving groups (especially in Turkey and Iran) and can be one of the most aesthetically dramatic and attractive of all kilim designs. However, the essential symmetry of a centralized design can be disturbed if one side of the kilim is placed too near to a wall or a large piece of furniture. This is especially critical with large, room-sized items – where possible they should be placed in a central position, with the furniture evenly distributed on all four sides. Good results can also be achieved by putting one side a few feet from the wall and the opposite side approximately the same distance from a large piece of furniture. Centralized designs also make ideal wall-hangings.

Vertical and horizontal designs (pls 10, 11, 37, etc.) The design runs one way along the kilim and, for optimum effect, needs to be viewed from one direction. Prayer rugs and pictorial schemes are common examples of these designs and make perfect wall-hangings. If used on the floor, try to place these designs where they cannot be seen upside down (e.g., with the top end against a wall).

Size and shape

Selecting the correct size of kilim requires more than simply ensuring that it fits the available space. All kilims should have a degree of breathing space and the more dramatic the colours and design, the greater the space needed to make sure that they are neither cramped by their surroundings nor overpower everything else in the room. This is especially important with room-sized items – consideration also needs to be given to any items required to fit into a specific space or to those where doors need to be opened across them. Remember that fringes are not usually included in the measurements – a 12' x 3' (3.7 x 0.9 m) runner may, for example, be up to an extra foot in length.

Traditional kilim sizes Frequently governed by local conventions that relate to their intended functions and are often incompatible with the optimum requirements of floor-coverings in the West. However, many kilims are now produced in Western sizes and, with a little flexibility and imagination, even traditional shapes and sizes can be adapted to conform to Western furnishing demands. (*See* Shapes and sizes, p. 30)

Function and location

In addition to purely decorative considerations, it is also important to remember that certain types of kilim are more suited to some functions and locations than others. For example, a lightweight, pastel-coloured kilim may be perfect for a bedroom or lounge, but may not stand up as well to heavy traffic as a darker, heavier duty item would. It is therefore advisable to choose runners or kilims that will be located in busy rooms or near doors for their extra durability in addition to their appearance.

Hanging kilims Can give a room a dramatic focal point and are also an ideal way of protecting old or worn items from further wear and tear and exhibiting prayer-rug, pictorial and other designs that need to be seen from one direction. Kilims may be hung directly against a wall (provided it is not too damp), suspended in front of alcoves, doorways, wardrobes or even used as room dividers. Many kilims were originally produced as hangings (*see* Chapter II) and provided they hang reasonably evenly, and are of a manageable size, the process is fairly straightforward and can produce excellent results. Kilims can be hung using a number of different methods:

Traditional kilim floor arrangement

Carpet grips are narrow strips of wood or metal with small pins protruding from one side, which are used to fit wall-to-wall carpets. This method is ideal – provided that the kilim is not too large or heavy – and enables easy removal and replacement. It simply requires a strip, approximately one inch shorter than the width of the kilim, to be attached (by screws or masonry nails) to a wall at a height corresponding to the top of the kilim. Make sure that the pins are pointing outwards and upwards and then just press the kilim against the pins.

The rod and sleeve method involves sewing a cotton sleeve along the top of the kilim on the reverse side. A metal or wooden rod, at least two inches wider than the kilim, can then be inserted into the sleeve and attached to the ceiling or alcove walls by the appropriate type of brackets. Heavy kilims can be supported by additional brackets. This method is time consuming and only suitable for kilims that hang evenly and are symmetrical and rectangular.

Curtain tape and hooks can be used in exactly the same way as they are for hanging curtains (drapes), but they are only recommended for lightweight, regularly shaped items that hang evenly.

Wooden beading, approximately one inch shorter than the kilim, can be attached to the top on the reverse side by stapling, tacking or sewing through pre-drilled holes. It can be suspended by means of a wire, fishing line or string (preferably translucent), from hooks or brackets fixed to the ceiling, alcove or wall.

Perspex and glass can be used to mount small kilims or kilim fragments, either by fitting them into a conventional clip frame or sandwiching them between two sheets of perspex or glass. Alternatively, they can be mounted by drilling a number of tiny holes into a single sheet of perspex and sewing the kilim through the holes with an appropriately coloured thread. Different-coloured sheets of perspex can create a variety of effects.

Framing kilims in the same way as oil paintings is also a possibility, especially for smaller, lightweight items. This method requires the construction of a wooden or metal frame with the same dimensions as the kilim; the kilim is then stretched over the frame and secured by pins, tacks or sewing. Artists' stretcher frames are ideal as they have small wedges that can be tapped to varying depths into the four corners of the frame after the kilim has been attached, ensuring that it stretches tightly and evenly. The kilim can then be mounted on the wall, with or without a surrounding frame.

Bags (pls 20, 23, 24, 38) Can be used for various purposes, depending on size, shape and durability, and often require little or no modification other than attaching straps or sewing on zips or other fasteners.

Cushions of various sizes and shapes can be made from all bags except the smallest – they only need to be filled with cushions or pieces of foam. The open end can then be secured by a zip, toggles, hooks and eyes, velcro or some other form of fastener.

Small bags are suitable for use as purses, vanity bags and handbags, provided they are fitted with shoulder straps or handles. If the original straps are missing, they can be easily replaced by sewing appropriately coloured cord on to the sides. Alternatively, short strips of webbing or some other strong fabric can be sewn on to both the front and back of the bag to form a pair of handles. The fitting of zips, velcro or other fastenings provides extra security.

Large bags are ideal for storing anything from clothes to children's toys and can be attached with a length of cord (which can double up as a shoulder strap) to a wall or the inside of a wardrobe. They can also be adapted for use as holdalls or sports bags by the addition of handles, fasteners and, perhaps, internal compartments sewn on the inside.

Saddle-bags can be draped over a rail or bannister and used as double-sided storage bags or magazine racks. Seats can also be produced by filling both compartments with cushions and then propping one compartment up vertically against a wall or chair frame and leaving the flat against the floor.

Artefacts and trappings (pl 22) Can be displayed in a number of ways, either as wall decorations or attached along the edges of tables, chairs, sofas, mirrors, etc., to serve as highly decorative protective trims.

Other uses Kilims may also be used as tablecloths, bedspreads and furniture covers, depending on their size and shape. Damaged items can be cut and used to make bags, cushions, pillowcases or a number of other useful furnishings and artefacts. (*See* Kilims for special purposes, p. 31)

Small runners can be sewn together at the sides to form attractive bolster cushions or long pillows for beds or sofas.

Assessing quality

Assessing the quality of a kilim is primarily a combination of careful observation and common sense – with a little basic information and experience, anyone should be able to distinguish between a good and a poor quality item. The most important step is to recognize that quality is always a mixture of subjective and objective criteria. However, even subjective assessment needs to be tempered because if you hope to re-sell, it is important that your personal tastes coincide with more generally held views of what constitutes an attractive kilim. Objective criteria include the integrity of the weave, the quality of the materials and the clarity and permanence of the dyes along with whether or not the kilim lies flat and evenly on the floor. There are a few basic tests, but, to some degree, the overall quality of a kilim always has to be taken on trust.

Assessing the suitability of the materials You should try to gage the general health of the wool by running your finger across the surface and then squeezing sections of the kilim to test if it springs back into shape. Good wool is supple and does not crease easily and, if your fingers become a little greasy, it indicates the presence of natural lanolin (and other vital oils). However, if the kilim feels hard and dry there is a possibility that poor quality wool has been used, or that the natural oils have been lost due to bad storage conditions, or excessive chemical washing. It is also useful to tug at the kilim, both lengthways and widthways, in order to check the tensile strength of the warp and weft. However, most kilims on the market today are made of good quality materials and, provided they are not subjected to excessive wear and tear, should last for many years.

Assessing the integrity of the weave Requires some knowledge of the different flatweaving techniques, but a simple test is to hold a section of the kilim up to the light, pull it slightly in opposite directions and note the amount of space between the weave. A tight weave will show very little, if any, discernible space between the warp and weft, whereas a loose weave will have sizeable gaps. Tightly woven kilims are generally more compact and durable than those with looser weaves. However, it is important to remember that some weaving techniques produce intrinsically tighter weaves than others and one can effectively only compare like with like, i.e., *soumak* with *soumak* or slitweave with slitweave.

Assessing the clarity and permanence of the dyes Largely a matter of trusting both your own initial impression of the kilim's appearance and the reputation of the specific weaving group. Detailed chemical analysis can be performed in a laboratory, but this is an expensive and generally unnecessary process normally reserved for dating old and antique items. The vast majority of modern dyes, whether natural or synthetic, are both attractive and permanent and, apart from a degree of natural mellowing, will remain colourfast throughout the life of the kilim. Consequently, if the colours look good at the outset, they will probably not deteriorate with age. Equally, if they appear dull and lacklustre, they are unlikely to improve. Colour irregularities (*abrashes*) are common in tribal items and, provided they are not too severe, do not detract from the kilim's value.

Assessing whether or not a kilim lies flat Simply place the kilim on a flat, even surface and then walk around and across it until you have viewed and walked over it from every direction. Always look from just a few inches above the floor because some ridges and troughs may not be visible from above, and then run your hands across the surface to detect any bumps or unevenness you may have missed. A degree of unevenness is acceptable both in tribal and in some regional items and will not necessarily detract from the kilim's value, although excessive unevenness generally makes any item less desirable and more difficult to position, either on the floor or the wall. (*See* Chapter II for more detailed information on materials, dyes and weaving techniques.)

Dating and attribution

Determining exactly when an undated kilim was made is virtually impossible unless its provenance has been systematically recorded, which is extremely rare. Consequently, the dating of most old and antique items is a matter of opinion. A number of factors are normally taken into account (design, colour scheme, weave, size, shape, type of dyes, etc.). However, experts of equal merit have been known to disagree over the century of production (although a consensus within two or three decades is more common) and it may be impossible to obtain even a generally agreed probable date. Chemical analysis of the fibres and dyes can assist in establishing a more reliable date of manufacture, but even this is not always foolproof and it is advisable to treat all dating with a degree of scepticism.

Dates and signatures May be woven into the fabric of a kilim, but should not be taken as conclusive proof of when and by whom it was made. Deliberate forgery is extremely rare, but reproducing older items is normal practice and it is not uncommon for illiterate weavers simply to copy the date or signature as part of the design. They may also make mistakes when weaving letters and numbers or may just treat them as motifs that can be adapted to enhance the design. Consequently one should be wary of accepting the authenticity of a dated kilim unless it conforms to other criteria that would place it in the same period.

Reading dates This is fairly straightforward because they are usually written in either European or, more frequently, Arabic numerals (which are read from right to left), and conform to the Muslim, Gregorian or Julian calendar systems. The Muslim calendar, which begins on 16 July 622 is the one predominantly found on kilims throughout most of the weaving region. The Gregorian or Western calendar is used by Christian Armenians and a few other weaving groups, although a number of older items from these groups were dated according to the almost identical Julian calendar, which was used in Russia until replaced, in 1918, by the Gregorian system.

Converting the Muslim calendar to the Western (Gregorian) year requires a fairly simple calculation. First divide the date on the kilim by 33 – because the Muslim year is approximately $\frac{1}{33}$ (or 11 days) shorter than the Gregorian year – subtract the result from the original date and then add this figure to 622 (the date of Mohammed's flight from Mecca to Medina) to find the Gregorian (or Western) year. For example, a kilim dated 990 would be calculated as follows: 990 - 33 = 30; 990 - 30 = 960; 960 + 622 = 1582.

Age classification Varies slightly from country to country, but, as a general rule, anything made in the last 20 to 30 years is considered to be contemporary; earlier this century 'old'; and during the 19th century or before 'antique'.

The relationship between colours and age Colours fade (or mellow) with prolonged exposure to light – the older a kilim is, the greater the probability of its colours having faded. However, it is extremely dangerous to jump to the conclusion that a kilim must be old because its colours have begun to fade – chemical washing and short-term exposure to strong light can produce the same effects very quickly. (*See* Chapter II)

Attributions Exact attributions of kilims can be extremely difficult to obtain, even from experts in the field, because many kilims from different weaving groups may look very similar. Also, some shop assistants make incorrect attributions due to their ignorance of the subject. Deliberate deception is extremely rare, but it is not unknown even though every country has its own laws pertaining to trading standards and these apply to the sale of kilims. As a general rule, you should judge each item on its individual merits, rather than when, where or by whom it might have been made.

What to pay

The amount you pay should be determined by what you can afford and the market cost of obtaining something that is adequate for your needs. It is not unknown for people to be swayed by the salesman's patter or swept along by the atmosphere of an auction, only to realize afterwards that they have overspent their budget. Equally, people sometimes buy an expensive kilim when a cheaper, more functional item would be more suitable.

Shopping around Always advisable because prices can vary considerably between local retail outlets – you may find discrepancies of between 20% and 40% for almost identical items sold in the same country, town or even the same street. Take your time when looking at individual kilims and do not be afraid to mention that you are considering buying from another retail outlet – the fear of losing a sale to a rival may have a favourable effect on the asking price. Also make a list of possible items and compare the prices being asked at different outlets – remembering to compare only items of the same size, origin and quality.

Home trials Offered by a number of retail outlets, usually as either straightforward loan periods or as a sale with a money-back guarantee if returned within a specified time. Both provide the chance to view the kilim in context and are always worth considering, especially if buying for a specific location or function.

Flexible pricing Common in most retail outlets, with the possible exception of department stores, and dealers are usually prepared to bargain. However, there is always a lower limit below which the dealer will not or cannot go and it is useful to have some idea of the minimum prices being asked in other retail outlets for kilims of the same type, size and origin before negotiations start. The degree of flexibility can vary considerably between different retail outlets – some work on the premise that 'starting high' and then giving large discounts will make the customer feel they have secured a real bargain; others prefer to start low, engaging the prospective buyer's interest from the outset, and then give a smaller discount as a gesture of goodwill. However, it is always the final selling price and not the initial starting price that really matters. Skilled bargaining can result in similar selling prices being agreed across a range of outlets whose starting prices were extremely diverse.

Price and value

Kilim prices are determined by a number of factors, some of which relate directly to the intrinsic merits of individual items and some of which are purely commercial in origin. The latter include purchase in the country of origin, shipping, washing, import tariffs, exchange rates and tax. These can vary quite considerably – not only between producing countries, but also between respective producing and importing nations – and there will always be some discrepancy in the relative prices of items of comparable quality, depending on where they were made and where they are sold.

Worldwide fluctuations in price Usually the result of increases or decreases in either the costs of production or the number of rugs being exported from individual producing countries – normally as the result of war, revolution, political or economic instability or a reversal of domestic policies. Price changes affecting all producing countries are usually caused by alteration in the cost or availability of raw materials (e.g., wool).

National fluctuations in price Mainly influenced by variations in the standards of living, exchange rates or import tariffs, and the political relationships of individual producing or importing nations. For example, a number of importing countries (most notably the USA) impose vastly different import tariffs, which range from 0% to 40%, depending on how they view the political regime in the producing country. Thus any alteration in the nature of the regime (e.g., a transition from communism to democracy) or how it is viewed (e.g., because of a change in foreign policy or a new political administration) can dramatically alter the import costs. For example, the average costs of production in Turkey are generally higher than in Afghanistan which makes Turkish kilims slightly more expensive to buy at source. However, the variable costs of shipping, import tariffs and exchange rates can even out or reverse the price differentials. The relative standards of living in individual importing countries also influence the selling price and, at any given time, for example, the same kilim may be more expensive in Sweden than in Germany or vice versa.

Local fluctuations in price Usually the result of differing overheads and profit margins of rival retail outlets. It is also common practice for certain kilims to be used as 'loss leaders' and, if these coincide with your requirements, it is possible to obtain a kilim at a substantially reduced cost. Similarly, an individual retail outlet may obtain a consignment of kilims on exceptionally favourable terms and be able to pass these savings on to their customers. Some retail outlets may also decide to offset any temporary surfeit of kilims, or lack of sales, or increases in import costs by reducing their profit margins or selling items imported before the less favourable conditions came into force. It is, however, equally possible that other retail outlets might decide to sell any stock bought before a decrease in wholesale costs for as near as possible to their original retail price before releasing their newer, cheaper stock. Large wholesalers, and some retailers, often have kilims in their warehouses for many years before putting them on the market. Some retail outlets will generally operate on a high turnover, low profit margin and minimal service basis; whereas others tend to opt for lower turnover, higher profit margins and more comprehensive customer service.

Price and quality Not always closely connected. The varying costs of import and production can result in good quality items from one country being cheaper than medium quality items from another. Also the prices of tribal and regional kilims are often more influenced by rarity and collectability than technical quality. However, there is some truth in the maxim that 'you get what you pay for' and exceptional kilims are usually more expensive than more ordinary items from the same group or of the same general type. Contemporary workshop items, however, are normally priced according to their quality, e.g., standard or superior and sometimes employ separate generic names (e.g., Oudzem and Tiffelt) to band different quality items from the same general source.

Cost and size Related to each other to the extent that larger kilims from a similar source are normally more expensive, but, unlike pile rugs (which are often sold by the m² or ft²), there is not usually an intrinsic connection between price and size. As a general rule, tribal and regional kilims are sold as individual pieces and priced according to their particular merits, rather than their size. With contemporary workshop items, price and size are much more closely related.

The price of old and antique items Normally based on a combination of rarity, collectability and general condition.

Price comparisons

Fixing kilims' cash prices is impossible because, regardless of their accuracy at the time of writing, the inevitable fluctuations in both production and import costs would soon render them out of date. However, provided allowances are made for any dramatic changes (e.g., war or natural disasters) in a specific producing country or region it is possible to fix the average price of items from one weaving group in relation to another. For example, Turkish regional kilims from Kayseria, Mut and Esme are all roughly the same price; regional kilims from the Senneh, in Iran, are approximately 50% more expensive; and Maimana kilims, from Afghanistan, cost slightly less. Similarly, Belouch kilims are

generally the same price as those produced by Lurs, Aimaq and a number of other tribal weaving groups, but generally less expensive than Afshar and Shahsavan tribal weavings. These price differentials do not, however, take into account local variations based on the popularity of particular kilims or supply and demand – popular items (especially if scarce) may be slightly more expensive than unpopular ones.

Choosing a yardstick Necessary to create a simple and effective system of comparison. Kilims from almost any weaving group could be used, but it is helpful if those chosen are both popular and distinctive, so assuring a reasonable chance of widespread availability and enabling relatively easy recognition. If we therefore take a standard Afghan Belouch kilim as a yardstick, a reasonable indication of the price of kilims from other weaving groups can be given in terms of plus or minus 'x' percent. For example, a kilim retailing for approximately the same price would be marked 0%; one costing about 40% more would be +40%; and one averaging 20% less -20%.

Some weaving groups produce kilims of a fairly standard quality, so their cost differentials normally vary little. Others make items that range considerably in quality and price and may, therefore, oscillate between 10% and 50% of the yardstick differentials and some contemporary workshop groups produce both standard and superior items under the same generic name.

Comparing items from different producing countries is difficult because variations in local production costs and the disparity in exchange rates and import tariffs between all the importing and exporting countries can distort the relative retail prices. For example, Belouch kilims sold in Afghanistan are generally slightly less expensive than comparable items exported from Iran. However, even allowing for slight discrepancies, these price comparisons provide a useful indication of comparative costs.

Note Old and antique rugs must be judged individually and cannot be included in these comparisons.

Price categories

Kilims can be banded into low, medium and high cost price categories. Items made by some weaving groups may straddle the boundary between two categories and standard and superior items produced by the same group may be found in separate categories. Also, exceptional or inferior items from any group may fall into a higher or lower category.

Low category items Generally cost the same amount or less than the yardstick. These include: Ardebil, Azerbaijan, Bakhtiari, Harsin, Khamseh, Khorassan, Kurdish (tribal), Luri, Meshed, and Shiraz/Qashga'i from Iran; and Esme, Fethiye, Kayseria, Konya, Mut and standard grade contemporary workshop items from Turkey; most regional and contemporary workshop items from Afghanistan and Morocco fall into this category; and also, standard grade contemporary workshop items from the Balkans and the former Soviet Caucasian Republics.

Medium category Generally cost up to 50% more than the yardstick. These include: Afshar, Bidjar, Qashga'i, Senneh, Shahsavan, Veramin and superior quality tribal and regional items from Iran; Bergama, Konya, Obruk, Sarkoy, Sivas, Van and a number of other items from regional groups, as well as most superior grade items from contemporary weaving groups in Turkey; some tribal items from Afghanistan and Morocco; and also, superior grade workshop items from the Balkans, and a number of tribal and regional kilims from the former Soviet Republics of the Caucasus and Central Asia.

High category items Normally cost over 50% more than the yardstick. These include: old and antique kilims and exceptional items from the medium price category groups.

Approximate price comparisons between groups

Afghanistan	Maimana/Labijar	-60/-40%	**Morocco**	Azrou	-40/0%
	Taimani/Aimaq	-20/+10%		Oudzem (standard workshop)	-60/-40%
Armenia	regional	0/+50%		Tiffelt (superior workshop)	-20/0%
	workshop	-30/0%		Zaiane	-10/0%
				Zemmour	-60/-30%
Azerbaijan	(Caucasus) regional	-20/+40%			
	workshop	-30/0%	**Romania**	regional	0/+40%
				standard workshop	-40/-30%
				superior workshop	0/+40%
Bulgaria	standard workshop	-30/+40%			
	superior workshop	0/+40%	**Turkey**	standard workshop (Ushak, Izmir, etc.)	-60/-40%
Iran	Afshar	+20/50%		superior workshop (Ushak, Izmir, etc.)	0/+50%
	Ardebil	-60/-40%		Esme/Fethiye/Kayseria/Mut (workshop)	-40/+20%
	Bakhtiari	-50/0%		Konya	-20/+20%
	Bidjar	-20/+20%		Sarkoy	-20/+30%
	Harsin	-60/-30%		Van	-10/+20%
	Khorassan	-20/+20%			
	Meshed	-30/-10%	**Turkoman**	Tekke	0/+30%
	Qashga'i (tribal)	0/+40%		Yomut	-20/+20%
	Senneh	0/+30%			
	Shahsavan	+10/40%			
	Shiraz/Qashga'i	-50/-20%			
	Veramin	-10/+40%			

Where and when to buy

There are several types of retail outlet in Europe, America, Australasia and the Far East, each offering slightly different advantages and disadvantages. No specific kind of outlet has a monopoly on either quality or value for money and genuine bargains may be found in all. It is therefore advisable to shop around, ignore any attempt by one outlet to put you off visiting others or persuade you that some types of outlet are intrinsically better than others. As with other areas of commerce, there is often a wide discrepancy in the level of knowledge, helpfulness and integrity of individuals in each type of outlet and if you have established a good relationship with one outlet it may be advisable to stay with them provided they have the right kilim at the right price.

Specialist shops Usually have a wide selection of kilims in different sizes, designs and styles and allow you time to examine individual items at your leisure, sometimes including home trials. You can normally contact them if you have any problems or require further advice. The staff are generally reasonably knowledgeable, although sometimes their knowledge is limited to the purely commercial aspects of the business. The main disadvantage of specialist shops is normally cost. They are often located in prestigious locations and carry extensive stocks, resulting in relatively high overheads, which must be passed on to the customer.

Department stores Some operate a franchise system, whereby their oriental rug and kilim department is run totally independently, so they are, in effect, exactly the same as specialist shops. Others sell kilims directly and can be divided into those selling a few kilims in addition to machine-made carpets and those that run their own specialist oriental rug and kilim department. The former normally carry a very limited stock, the prices are fixed and their staff usually have a minimal knowledge of the subject. However, they can be a useful source of reasonably priced furnishing items. Stores that have specialist departments usually have the same advantages and disadvantages as specialist shops, with the added bonus that credit facilities are normally available.

Auctions An exciting and unpredictable method of buying; excellent bargains can be had, but, unless you know something about the subject, you can just as easily pay too much. It is therefore advisable to do your homework – choose the type and size of kilim you want and then check the prices of similar items in a range of retail outlets. Also try to familiarize yourself with the procedure and atmosphere of an auction prior to buying by attending one or two beforehand and never be afraid to ask the auctioneer how the bidding is to be regulated, whether there are reserves (a price below which an item will not be sold) and if there are any additional charges on top of the hammer price. It is normal for tax and, sometimes, a buyer's premium (usually 10 to 15%) to be added to the successful bid.

Never be too concerned about the reasons put forward for an auction because regardless of whether the sale is a result of a liquidation, or private individuals selling their collections, or simply a company trying to move its surplus stock, the basic dynamics remain the same. Thus the auctioneer will try to obtain the highest possible price for his clients and the audience will endeavour to pay as little as possible for each item. Remember that your chances of getting a bargain are mainly determined by the interest shown in each item by rival bidders and the auctioneer's (or vendor's) willingness to set reasonable reserves. Always be sceptical about claims of 'no reserves' as this may be true for some items, but auctioneers have a responsibility to their clients and are unlikely to sell valuable items for 10% or 20% of their normal retail price.

The main disadvantage of auctions is that you have to make an instant decision and pay in full at the end. However, it is usual to have a viewing period prior to the auction when you have the opportunity to ask questions and examine the kilims to be sold. Some auctioneers may be willing to change items if they prove to be the wrong size, colour or design – although this is entirely at their discretion and depends on the specific instructions they have received from the vendor.

Auctioneers have to abide by strict rules governing the conduct of auctions, in addition to more general trading regulations. These may vary from country to country, but normally anyone buying at an auction will be protected by law if they purchase a kilim that is faulty or sold under a false description. Auctioneers normally point out any faults before taking bids and, although mistakes in cataloguing and attribution do occur, auction houses are normally too protective of their reputations to consider blatant deceptions. However, it is important to remember that attributions of age and provenance are usually only opinions – especially with old and antique items – and the auction house cannot be held liable for errors unless deliberate deception is intended.

Ethnic shops Normally sell a wide range of ethnic artefacts (masks, sculptures, shadow puppets, clothes, jewelry, etc.) in addition to kilims and, like department stores, can be divided into those that sell a few kilims as part of their general stock and those that have a specialist kilim section. The former normally have a limited range, usually of standard quality contemporary workshop items and may be a useful source of attractive and reasonably priced furnishing items. The latter offer many of the same advantages as specialist shops, but generally tend towards tribal items and may not have quite as extensive a collection of contemporary workshop and the more expensive regional items. However, the owners often have a genuine interest in the subject – sometimes visiting the producing countries and selecting individual items themselves – and the shops are frequently located in less prestigious locations, allowing their lower overheads to be passed on to the customer.

Exhibitions These are set up in the same way as art exhibitions – the kilims are displayed in a gallery or some other suitable location for a week or two and the public are invited to view and (if they wish) purchase anything on display. They are usually organized either by kilim dealers who do not have a retail outlet or by specialist shops who want a short-term outlet in another location. Their advantages and disadvantages are similar to those of auctions, although without the bidding and with a longer time to make a choice.

Private sales Not usually covered by the laws governing commercial sales and, although specific regulations vary from country to country, generally the buyer has limited legal protection. Private sales, however, can still be worth considering because bargains can be had. It is, though, often a good idea to obtain a professional valuation, especially for more expensive items because it provides both the buyer and the seller with a reasonable market price and limits the likelihood of future recriminations. However, if the seller is a private dealer then normal trading regulations and taxation will usually apply to any sale. Private dealers offer many of the advantages of specialist shops and can be useful in locating unusual or hard-to-find kilims, but, unless you know them personally or by reputation, there is always a chance that they may disappear if problems arise.

Catalogues and mail order Both can be useful for people who are unable to visit a retail outlet in person, but it is impossible to assess quality from a photograph, so these methods of buying can only be recommended if there is a money-back guarantee.

Markets and antique shops A useful, but unreliable, method of purchase. Bargains can be found, but most non-specialist traders know very little about the subject and they are just as likely to overcharge as undercharge.

Buying in countries of origin Can be hazardous. Kilims are not always cheaper in their producing country (especially after import tax and shipping costs have been added), but bargains can be obtained and there is something special about having a memento of your visit. Buying in most countries is fairly straightforward, but – unless you carry the kilim with you – there is always a risk that it will not arrive at your home or that you will receive another (possibly inferior) item in its place. This does not happen very often, but if it does there is very little you can do. It is important to remember that most retail outlets are geared to tourism and charge tourist prices (although hard bargaining or visiting more remote places may enable you to buy something for considerably less) and that some countries, Turkey in particular, have strict laws about exporting national treasures, which may include some old or exceptional kilims.

Buying rugs in other countries in the West Always worth considering because some kilims may be cheaper than at home, even allowing for import tariffs and the extra cost of shipping. Remember that some countries apply import tariffs relating to where the item was bought, others to where it was made: for example, an American citizen buying an Afghan kilim in Britain would have to pay the Afghan import tariff, rather than the one applied to British goods. So it is always advisable to find out from your own customs which of these criteria apply.

Choosing the best time to buy May cause more inconvenience than any financial saving might be worth, but, where possible, try to buy when supply is outstripping demand. This is usually indicated by a surfeit of sales, auctions and special offers; favourable market conditions can also be revealed by visiting selected retail outlets over a few weeks and noting any fluctuation in prices. Periodically, kilims from some countries may be disproportionately less expensive than items of similar quality from others. Also, different retail outlets might have loss leaders or an inexpensively obtained consignment.

Insuring kilims Always a good idea. Less expensive items can be included on a general household policy, but separate cover is recommended for more expensive ones. Keep photographs and descriptions of all your kilims and be sure to obtain a valuation – either when you buy or (for a small fee) from an accredited valuer at a later date. Remember that the insurance valuation is not the price you paid, but the replacement cost, which is normally more.

Where and when to sell

Resale value Depends on a number of factors, including, condition, origin, collectability and the market. Most retail outlets, with the possible exception of department stores, may be interested in buying a kilim directly or acting as agents – either on a commission basis or a flat fee basis.

The condition of a kilim is important in determining both the potential selling price and where to sell. Most specialist shops and auction houses are only interested in items that are in good condition and, unless a kilim has exceptional 'collectable' interest, it is a waste of time approaching them with anything that shows substantial wear and tear. However, even badly worn or damaged items may be of interest to private individuals or ethnic shops and private dealers, who make kilim bags from damaged items.

The origin of a kilim also governs who is likely to buy it. Generally, specialist shops, auction houses and ethnic shops are only interested in tribal and regional items. Some of these outlets may consider contemporary workshop items, but normally private sales are a better option.

Collectability is extremely hard to predict and often has little connection with the respective qualities of the different items available. However, at any given time, kilims of certain types or origins are likely to be more popular (and consequently more expensive) than others, so if possible try to sell a kilim when similar items are in fashion. Normally, only tribal and regional kilims become collectable, although exceptional contemporary workshop items may also be of interest to either private collectors or retail outlets, which specialize in the more sophisticated end of the market.

Old or unusual items are frequently of interest to specific collectors and if you have a kilim that falls into this category you could try to locate a buyer via a dealer, specialist shop or auction house.

Market conditions Influence the selling price of kilims generally and, if possible, try to approach a sale when the prices in the shops are high and demand is outstripping supply. Follow the same research procedures as when buying, but look for a steady rise in prices of kilims that belong to the same weaving group as the one you wish to sell.

Selling to a specialist shop The simplest way to dispose of a kilim, but expect to be paid considerably less than the anticipated retail price. Specialist shops can also act as agents – selling on your behalf at a fixed percentage, rather buying directly – but, you will probably wait longer for a sale. Old and antique items are best sold through outlets that attract established collectors.

Selling by auction Always has an element of chance, which can be substantially reduced by fixing a reasonable reserve. Some auction houses charge the vendor – either a flat fee or a percentage of the hammer price – while others cover their costs solely from the buyer's premium. Most specialist auction houses will only be interested in tribal and regional items, but general auctioneers may be a useful outlet for contemporary workshop kilims.

Selling privately Useful option for standard contemporary workshop items – whether tribal or regional – but not advisable for more expensive and potentially collectable items unless an independent valuation has been obtained so that both parties are aware of the general market price.

Care and repair

Kilims are extremely durable, but they are not indestructible and proper care and attention is necessary to maximize the life and appearance of your kilim. Wool is a superb material, but normal wear and tear, central heating, air conditioning and a number of household chemicals can have a detrimental effect on the fabric. However, a few simple precautions should ensure that your kilim lasts for many years.

Correct underlay Necessary to protect your kilim from damage caused by continually squeezing the fibres between the soles of your shoes and the floor. Always place a kilim on a carpeted floor or use an underlay – preferably one made from solid sponge rubber (not foam or ripple rubber, which are less suitable) or one produced from jute and animal hair coated with rubber on both sides.

Cleaning Important at regular intervals. Always work slowly and start by removing the surface dust with a carpet sweeper or vacuum cleaner (preferably one without beater bars, which might damage the fabric) and then shake the kilim gently to dislodge more ingrained dirt. Old, expensive or damaged items should be cleaned professionally.

Shampooing Puts some essential moisture back into the fibres, as well as removing more entrenched areas of grit and dirt. Start after the kilim has been cleaned and use a good quality wool detergent (which is usually also compatible with cotton and silk), with perhaps a cup of diluted vinegar and dab (never rub) it gently and evenly across the entire surface of the kilim. Then dry the kilim carefully and systematically, preferably by leaving it out in the sun. You should always check that there are no pockets of dampness, which can be removed by using a hand-held hair dryer. Old, expensive and delicate items should be cleaned by an oriental rug specialist – never by general cleaning companies who often use chemicals that can damage the fabric.

Removing stains Needs to be done carefully by dabbing (never rubbing) in order to prevent the colours from running. Always use a cleaning solution that is compatible with the material (i.e., wool, cotton or silk) and suitable for removing the specific stain (coffee, grease, etc.). Remove as much of the discolouring substance as possible and then dry the area carefully. There are a number of books that list the cleaning agents best suited to removing specific stains and several manufacturers are willing to give advice on how to remove stains caused by their products. However, if the stain persists or if the kilim is valuable or delicate consult a specialist cleaner.

Repairs Serious damage to the body of a kilim should be repaired by professionals, particularly on older or more expensive items, but minor damage can be rectified by sewing the affected area using matching coloured wool or appropriate material.

Additional maintenance measures Insect damage can largely be avoided by regular shampooing and mothproofing. Localized fading and uneven wear and tear is usually the result of not moving your kilim around to ensure that other parts of the surface are exposed to bright sunlight or heavy traffic. Alternatively, you can periodically put your kilim in storage, e.g., during the summer if fading is a problem. This should preferably be done after first having it cleaned, shampooed and mothproofed and then covering both sides with polythene and rolling it into a tight cylindrical form. Also make sure that houseplants are never placed directly on the floor near a kilim because mildew (a type of fungus) can infect and damage items containing cotton.

Meander border

CHAPTER IV

The cultural context

The kilim-weaving countries and their inhabitants have been in an almost constant state of flux for most of the last two millennia. Invasions, occupations, migrations, forced expulsions and resettlements have relocated different ethnic and cultural groups throughout an area that stretches from North Africa to western China. Empires have risen and fallen, ancient civilizations have flourished and declined, countries have been fragmented or absorbed into other nations; names and national boundaries have changed, and even today, with the recent dissolution of the Soviet Union, it is by no means certain that the current boundaries and the racial integrity of several of the emerging nations will remain secure.

All these changes have had, and will continue to have, a dramatic effect on the kilim-weaving people and the quantities, qualities, styles, types and designs of the kilims they produce, as well as the countries and regions in which they reside and work. It is therefore essential, if one hopes to gain some understanding of the subject, to familiarize oneself with the ethnic, religious and cultural backgrounds of the weavers, their movements throughout the entire kilim-producing territories and the way national boundaries have changed.

The weaving people

Today, kilim weaving is practised by people of many different ethnic and cultural origins. Some of the weavers are the indigenous inhabitants of the region in which they now live, others arrived – at different times during the last 2,000 years – via conquest or migration, bringing with them their own weaving traditions and cultural values. Over the centuries, varying degrees of assimilation have taken place, resulting in a gradual fusion of diverse traditions into the more homogeneous ones that we now associate with each individual country, region or weaving group.

In some areas, one culture or ethnic group became so politically and socially dominant that it gradually absorbed the cultural and weaving identities of all the other inhabitants of the region to the point where it is now no longer possible to detect any ethnic or cultural diversity in the kilims woven there today. In other areas several different ethnic and cultural groups (e.g., Kurds, Belouch) have retained their unique weaving traditions – frequently despite being politically and culturally subservient – and the kilims they produce now are often far closer in character and appearance to those woven by their kinsmen in other countries than they are to those woven in the next village by people of different ethnic origins.

Therefore, in order to understand the subject more fully, it is necessary to identify the major ethnic and cultural groups throughout the entire kilim-weaving area and to establish the major historical, religious and social factors that have forged the current demographic and cultural make-up of the kilim-weaving people and regions.

The major ethnic and cultural groups
Afghans Characteristically fair-skinned people, also known as Pathans (Pakhtuns or Pushtoons). They are the largest and the politically dominant ethnic group in Afghanistan – also found in substantial numbers in Pakistan and northern India. Afghans are composed of a number of traditionally nomadic and semi-nomadic tribal groups, including the Mohmands, Mangals and Wiziris (who claim descent from one of the lost tribes of Israel). They are mainly Sunnite Muslims who speak Pashto (a variant of Persian) and many still retain a largely nomadic and semi-nomadic lifestyle. The term Afghan is also used as a general description of any inhabitant of Afghanistan, regardless of their ethnic group.
Arabs People of Semetic origin who are the largest and politically dominant ethnic group in North Africa and the Middle East. They also

inhabit – often in isolated pockets – other parts of the weaving region. An Arab civilization is known to have existed, during the 2nd century BC, in the watered highlands of Yemen. It gradually extended its influence northwards and westwards through Saudi Arabia and the Nile Delta, but it was not until the 7th century (shortly after Mohammed's death) that Arab civilization, inspired by Islamic zeal, emerged as a major evangelical, political and cultural force.

The Arabs remained a minority racial and religious group until the 8th century when Arab colonization had been established throughout North Africa, the Middle East and Central Asia, and many of the subject peoples had been converted to Islam – no doubt encouraged to some degree by the tax, career and social advantages available to Muslims. Over the succeeding centuries, Arab political dominance was supplanted in most of its former territories by a number of different ethnic groups (Turks, Kurds, Berbers, Mongols, Persians), but they left behind a tremendous cultural and artistic legacy and also established Islam as the dominant religion throughout most of the kilim-weaving region. Today, 'ethnic' Arabs produce a significant number of kilims in several countries (especially in North Africa) – both as separate ethnic Arab weaving groups and also as part of multi-ethnic or trans-ethnic weaving groups.

Armenians Descended from a branch of Indo-Europeans who originally lived in a region of the Caucasus known as Armenia. They adopted Christianity in the 3rd century AD and are the only major ethnic group throughout the entire weaving region (outside the Balkans) to have retained their faith and resisted the pressures to convert to Islam. Today, ethnic Armenians can be found in Armenia, the other former Soviet Caucasian Republics and to a lesser extent Turkey, Iran, the Middle East, America and Europe.

There is some uncertainty regarding the exact origins of the Armenian people. The ancient Greek historian, Herodotus (c. 485–425 BC), believed that they were related to the ancient Phrygians, although most modern historians trace the beginnings of Armenian culture to the founding of the Urartian civilization in the 6th century BC. What is not in dispute, however, is that the Armenians established a civilization, during the 1st century BC, powerful enough to challenge the Roman Empire.

Since then their cultural, religious and racial integrity has not only survived over 2,000 years of conquest, subjugation, dispersal and persecution (culminating in the massacre and forcible expulsion of nearly 6 million ethnic Armenians by Turkey and Russia at the beginning of the 20th century), but also provided the world with a remarkable artistic legacy that has arguably found its finest expression in kilim and rug weaving. Today, Armenian weaving is largely confined to the Armenian Republic and the Nagorny Karabagh region of the Azerbaijan Republic, although its influence is found throughout the Middle East. Most Armenian weaving is regional/tribal in character and production.

Aryans (Indo-Europeans) Nomadic people who migrated from the Eurasian Steppes to the Indus and Nile valleys, during the 2nd millennium BC, and eventually settled in parts of the Middle East, Central Asia and north-west India. The entire Indo-European group of languages is derived from the language they spoke. Today, the term 'Aryan' is often used to describe northern Europeans (proto-Aryans), but should more correctly be applied to all Indo-European people, who include the Berbers, Kurds, Belouch, Persians (Iranians), Pathans (from Pakistan and Afghanistan) and most of the inhabitants of the Middle East, Asia Minor, Central Asia and northern India prior to the Turkic and Mongol invasions.

Azerbaijanis A relatively homogeneous ethnic group with Turkic origins who are now divided between the former Soviet Republic of Azerbaijan and the province of the same name in north-west Iran.

Note It is not always clear whether kilims marketed as 'Azerbaijans' were made by ethnic Azerbaijanis or whether they originated from Soviet or Iranian Azerbaijan. Most Soviet items are made by ethnic Azerbaijanis, but those from Iran may have been produced by members of different ethnic groups.

Bedouins Arabic-speaking nomadic herdsmen who occupy the predominantly desert regions of the Middle East. They operate a strict caste system of noble tribes, who can trace their ancestral origins, either to Qaysi (northern Arabia) or to Yamani (southern Arabia) and 'ancestorless' vassal tribes who live under the protection of the noble tribes. There are a number of authentic Bedouin kilims on the market, but the term is often used by dealers to describe the items produced by Arab weavers in general.

Berbers Indigenous inhabitants of the Maghrib (North Africa) who were given the name 'Barbari' by the Romans – meaning 'not Greek or Latin' and therefore uncivilized, coarse, cruel and barbarous – which was later modified to 'Berber'. There are a number of ethnic Berber weaving groups in Morocco, Algeria and Tunisia, and Berber influence can be seen in regional and contemporary workshop items throughout the region.

Georgians Indigenous Indo-European people who inhabit the Georgian Republic and, to a much lesser extent, the other former Soviet Caucasian Republics.

Medes Early Indo-European inhabitants of northern and central Iran – possibly of Armenoid (typical of Armenia) racial stock – who founded an empire centred around Hamadan (Ecbatana) in the north west of the country. They were later assimilated into the Persian population. (*See* Persians)

Mongoloids One of the five main racial divisions of *Homo sapiens* (Caucasian, Negro, etc.), which includes the indigenous people of eastern Siberia, China, South-East Asia and, some anthropologists believe, the continent of America. Often mistakenly referred to as Mongols.

Mongols Indigenous people of Mongolia, northern China and south-east Siberia – closely related to the Tibetans – who were traditionally nomadic herdsmen. Mongol society was based on allegiance to specific tribes (or clans), each under the leadership of a local Khan, and it was not until Genghis Khan (1162–1227) or 'Great Leader' united all the independent tribes and founded the Mongol empire, that a Mongolian nation could be said to exist. Today, small pockets of ethnic Mongols (e.g., the Borchalu in north-west Iran) and people of Mongol descent can be found in most of the countries along the original invasion route. (*See* Mongoloids)

Ottoman Turks (*See* Turks, Turkomen and the Turkic tribes)

Persians Early Indo-European inhabitants of southern Iran – possibly of Mediterranean racial stock – who conquered and assimilated the Medes. (*See* The Persian Empire, p. 53) Today, ethnic Persians (Medes/Persians) constitute about two-thirds of the population of Iran and are politically and culturally dominant.

Note In order to avoid confusion, the term 'Persian' will be used when discussing ethnic Persians and 'Iranian' when referring to inhabitants of Iran.

Timurids Used to describe the followers and descendants of Timur-the-Lame. (*See* Tamerlane, p. 55)

Turks, Turkomen and the Turkic tribes All derived from the name *Tu'kiu* or *T'uchueh*, which was given by the Chinese to nomadic tribesmen who, in the 6th century, founded an empire that stretched from Mongolia, through Siberia and northern Central Asia to the Black Sea. The name 'Turk', as it became, was then indiscriminately applied to anyone who came under their influence and is totally meaningless today as a racial term. It does, however, loosely connect a diverse group of tribal peoples – who ethnically seem to be a mixture of Alpine people from western Siberia, the Volga Basin and the Altai Mountains and Mongoloids from eastern Asia – through shared features of their history, traditions and language. Most of the Turkic tribes were involved in one of the Turko-Mongol (e.g., Seljuk, Ottoman, Genghis Khan) invasions that swept through Central Asia, the Middle East and eastern Europe from the 11th century onwards; others, particularly those in western Siberia and northern Central Asia, were probably either indigenous to the region or remnants of earlier *Tu'kiu* incursions.

Turks in Turkey are mainly descendants of the Seljuk Turks and the Ottoman Turks (both divisions of the main Oghuz or Ghuzz tribe), who conquered the country and established empires during the 11th and 13th centuries, respectively. The Seljuks' name is derived from Seljuk-ibn-Dakak, leader of the Kinik clan or sub-tribe. Similarly, the Ottomans were originally members of the Kayi clan or sub-tribe, who later adopted the name of their leader, Osman (or Uthman) and so are also sometimes referred to as the Osmalis. The Seljuks and the Ottomans established Islam as the state religion, absorbed or repressed the indigenous culture and population, and became the major political, cultural and ethnic force in modern Turkey. (*See* The Seljuk Empire, p. 54, and the Ottoman Empire, p. 55)

Turkomen are eastern Turks belonging to the south-western branch of the Turkic language group, who were almost exclusively nomadic until the early 20th century. They now live mainly in the Turkmenistan Republic and other former Soviet Central Asian Republics, although pockets can be found in Afghanistan, Iran, Turkey, Iraq and Syria. Turkomen are divided into a number of specific tribal groups (e.g., the Ersari, Yomut [Yomud], Tekke, Salor, Saryk and Chodor), each of which have a number of sub or associated, tribes (e.g., Arabatchi, Beshir and Kizyl Azak). However, dealers sometimes classify items produced by the Kazakhs, Kirghiz, Karakalpaks, Uzbeks, Uighurs and other Turkic peoples as Turkoman weavings.

Turkic tribes are generally defined as being social or ethnic groups, who speak one of the closely related Turkic languages, which, in common with Mongolian and Manchu-Tungus, are a sub-family of the Altaic language family. They are usually divided into the western branch, who occupy Europe, Turkey, north-west Iran and western Asia, and the eastern branch, who are found in former Soviet Central Asia, Afghanistan and the Sinkiang Province in China. Both branches contain people from a wide range of racial types, although the eastern Turks are predominantly dark skinned, and many Turkish Turks and Tartars are as fair skinned as Western Europeans. (*See* Chapter VII: Afshars, Azerbaijanis, Karakalpaks, Kazakhs, Kirghiz, Qashga'i, Tadjiks, Tartars, Turkomen, Turks, Uighurs and Uzbeks) *Note* Only those Turkic tribes that have a direct bearing on kilim weaving are discussed in this book.

Cultural influences

Despite their diverse ethnic origins, historical backgrounds and social evolution, the different kilim-weaving people share a number of unifying influences. The most important of which are tribal allegiance, the nomadic way of life and religion.

Tribal allegiance Evident not only in the use of overt tribal insignia (e.g., *guls*, *wasms*) by certain weaving groups, but also in the overall style and appearance of kilims made in the same tribal group, regardless of their geographical proximity. For example, Kurdish kilims, whether produced in eastern Turkey or in the Khorassan Province of Iran (nearly 1,000 miles to the east), are often unmistakably Kurdish in their overall character and appearance.

The nomadic way of life Had a profound effect on the kilim-weaving people – either because they evolved directly from a nomadic lifestyle or, at some time in their history, came under the influence of nomadic invaders (e.g., Turkic tribesmen). It is impossible to say with any degree of certainty whether the nomadic invaders introduced kilim weaving to certain areas or if they simply grafted their skills and conventions on to existing weaving traditions. There is no doubt that the nomadic way of life has had an abiding influence on the kilims produced throughout the entire weaving region.

Religious influences

Religious influences vary to some degree throughout the kilim-weaving region, but every weaving culture, at some point in its history, has been dominated by Islam – either through conquest or conversion. Islamic beliefs, symbolism and social conventions continue to be reflected in the kilims woven today. However, the influence of Islam within each individual national, ethnic or social group has been modified to varying degrees by earlier, or occasionally subsequent, religious doctrines. These modifying influences are clearly evident in the symbols, imagery and compositional format of their kilims. For example, some motifs (e.g., *boteh* and *herati*), common to Iranian kilims, are drawn from Zoroastrianism and pre-Islamic creation myths; traces of Christian imagery can be found on Armenian and Balkan items; Buddhist symbolism is often clearly discernible in East Turkestan weaving; and most tribal kilims still incorporate magical symbols that are a legacy of their earliest animistic beliefs.

Islam The dominant religion throughout the entire kilim-weaving region (except Armenia and the Balkans), founded by Mohammed (or Muhammad), who was born in Mecca (*c.* 570) and died in Medina (*c.* 632). Islam was first spread by Arab tribesmen during the 7th century and, by the 14th and 15th centuries, achieved dominance throughout the region via successive invasions, conquests and occupations – firstly, by the Arab Empire and later through waves of converted Mongol and Turkic tribesmen.

Mohammed lived most of his life in relative obscurity until around his 40th birthday when, while meditating in a cave at Hira (a hill near Mecca) during Ramadan (the month of heat), he fell into a trance and began to receive revelations from God. Followers of Islam consider

Mohammed to be the last in a line of prophets (who include Abraham and Christ) and he is often referred to simply as the Prophet.

The Koran (which means 'the reading') is the sacred book of Islam and is comprised entirely of the revelations given to the Prophet. It is divided into surahs or chapters, each relating to a specific set of revelations (e.g., Women, *Revealed at Al-Madinah*) and is taken as being the literal 'Words of God' by followers of Islam. It stresses the belief in one God (Allah) and, in common with Orthodox Judaism (with which it has much in common), concentrates on everyday behaviour and morality in which clear divisions are made between right and wrong.

The Hadith is a book of sayings and actions attributed to Mohammed when he was not in a trance and, although deeply influential on Islamic thought, the sayings are not taken as literal truths and are consequently open to different interpretations, e.g., the attitude towards the depiction of human/animal forms.

Islamic worship is based around the observance of five main duties: everyone, at least once in their life, must say with absolute conviction that 'There is no God but Allah and Mohammed is His Prophet'; pray, after ritually washing, facing in the direction of Mecca, five times a day – on rising, at noon, in mid-afternoon, after sunset and before retiring for the night; give alms generously and care for the sick and the poor; keep the fast of Ramadan (health permitting) by refraining from eating, drinking and indulging in worldly pleasures, between sunrise and sunset; make, if possible, the pilgrimage to Mecca.

The followers of Islam are generally referred to as Muslims or Moslems and may belong to one of a number of different sects – the most important of which are Sunnite, Shiite and Sufi.

Sunnite or Sunni Muslims are often referred to as orthodox Muslims and are members of the largest and most influential of the Islamic sects; dominating the majority of North Africa, Turkey, Afghanistan, Pakistan and the Soviet Central Asian and Soviet Caucasian Republics (with the exception of Armenia).

Shiite or Shia Muslims formed a breakaway sect shortly after the death of Mohammed, due to a dispute over the Prophet's successor. Today, Shiite Muslims are dominant in Iran and parts of the Middle East.

Sufi Muslims belong to a mystical, pantheistic sect of Islam, closely associated with the dervishes (Muslim friars or monks committed to a life of poverty and austerity) and responsible for some of the most profound and influential Islamic writing, art and metaphysical thought.

Christianity Far less influential than Islam, which it preceded by over 600 years. It was already established in the Balkans, Iran, Syria and many parts of the Middle East before successive Islamic invasions began to affect mass conversions; resulting in today's religious divisions. During the first few centuries after the death of Christ Christianity was divided along geographical and theological lines into numerous, often intensely hostile, movements or sects. The most important of which evolved into the Byzantine (or Eastern Orthodox), Armenian and Nestorian Churches.

The Byzantine Church challenged both the authority of the Pope and several aspects of Catholic doctrine and finally broke away from the See of Rome in around AD 1054. This division resulted in the establishment of the Eastern Orthodox Church, which included the former Byzantine patriarchates of Constantinople, Antioch, Alexandria and Jerusalem, as well as the national Churches of Greece, Russia, Romania, Bulgaria and Yugoslavia. Most of these areas (with the exception of Russia) were subsequently subjected to Islamic invasion and colonization and, in the kilim-producing regions (e.g., the Balkans), traces of Christian imagery were frequently incorporated into Islamic design conventions.

The Armenian (and Coptic) Churches, although generally considered to be part of the Eastern Christian Movement, rejected the authority and some of the orthodoxy of the Byzantine Church and even today are considered by the Orthodox Church to be a heretical sect.

Nestorian Christianity evolved from the doctrine of Nestorius (the 5th-century patriarch of Constantinople), who maintained that Mary should not be called the 'Mother of God' because she was only the mother of the 'human' and not the 'divine' aspect of Christ. It flourished in Iran and Syria, and small communities were also established in Afghanistan, India and China. Its influence was gradually replaced by that of Islam, but a Nestorian legacy can still be found throughout the region.

Mithraism and Zoroastrianism Pre-Christian religions that evolved in ancient Persia (Iran). They contained many of the basic doctrinal elements that would emerge at a later date in Christianity and which still exert an influence on Iranian culture and symbolism.

Mithra was the mythical god of light and truth, who (in common with Christ) came to earth via a miraculous birth, died and then rose from the dead. Mithra was also the central figure in a belief system that included: the constant fight between good and evil, heaven and hell, a last judgment and the immortality of the soul. It also recognized 25 December as the date of Mithra's birth, celebrated Easter and held Sunday to be a holy day. Mithraism was an essentially mystical religion, which excluded women and evolved around secret rites – using bells, holy water and candles – that were only known to devotees. It reached its height during the 2nd and 3rd centuries AD, becoming extremely popular with Roman soldiers, who spread its philosophy throughout the Empire and, even today, traces of Mithraic belief can be found throughout the Middle East, Asia and Europe.

Zoroastrianism was based on the teaching of Zarathustra (Zoroaster in Greek), who is believed to have lived sometime prior to the 6th century BC. Zoroastrianism is generally considered to be a purer, more sophisticated version of Mithraism, which it superseded as the dominant religion in Persia by the 3rd century AD. Zoroastrianism conceptualized the battle between good and evil into the figures of Ahura Mazda (god of light) and Ahriman (god of darkness) and stressed the importance of supporting, by actions as well as words, the forces of good. It flourished in Persia until the arrival of Islam, during the 7th century, which resulted in most Zoroastrians either converting to Islam or fleeing the country – mainly to India, where they are known as Parsees. Although Zoroastrianism as a religion was mainly confined to Persia, its teachings have had a profound effect on Christianity, Gnosticism, Judaism, Manichaeism and consequently, Islam and Buddhism.

Animatism and animism Collective names for belief systems that operate on the premise that all things, whether animate or inanimate, have a spirit, personality or lifeforce. These primitive beliefs, although dismissed as superstition by most major religions, nevertheless under-pin every facet of religious and magical symbolism and are the major inspiration behind a number of kilim motifs and designs.

Animatism holds that each object has its own individual spirit (known as 'soul substance' in China and 'manitou' among North American Indians), with its own specific powers and influences, which can be transferred to the individual or tribe.

Animism differs slightly from animatism, believing that objects do not have a spirit (or lifeforce) of their own, but that they can be occupied by gods, spiritual beings or souls of the dead, whose powers can then be harnessed and directed.

Invasions, migrations and empires

These are responsible for the spread and relocation of the different ethnic and cultural groups, as well as for the dissemination of religious, social and political ideas and institutions.

Early civilizations A number of Indo-European cultures, centred on Mesopotamia (the Tigris-Euphrates Valley) and the surrounding areas, probably existed as far back as the 9th and 10th centuries BC. Urban remains, dating from around 7,000 BC, were found at Jericho, but we know very little about this or other cultures in the region until the arrival of the Sumerians in around 4,000 BC. They were probably a Semitic people, who worshipped anthropomorphic gods, carried out sacrifices, wrote epic poetry and developed a practical understanding of how to apply geometric and algebraic problem-solving to urban construction. They were followed by a number of civilizations – most notably, the Akkadians (whose language was used as the lingua franca throughout the region before being replaced by Aramaic), Assyrians, Babylonians, Hittites, Kassites and Mitannis – who probably all had similar racial and cultural origins.

The Phoenicians inhabited the coastal region of Syria (Phoenicia) during the 2nd millennium BC. They invented a phonetic alphabet sometime before 1600 BC that became the forerunner of all European, Middle Eastern, Indian, South-East Asian, Ethiopian and Korean alphabets. They were active seafarers and traders, who made contacts with civilizations throughout Europe and Asia and were responsible for initiating many early cross-cultural influences.

India developed an urban civilization, by 3,000 BC – based around geometrically designed cities with underground sewers – which had its own writing system, highly developed arts and crafts and a 'fertility cult' religion. The people were probably ancestors of the Dravidians (the non-Aryan people of southern India and Sri Lanka – Tamils, Kanarese, etc.). During the period from 4,000 BC to 500 BC, the rest of the weaving region was inhabited by a number of Indo-European people – including the Scythians (north of the Black Sea), Urartus (Caucasus), Lydians (Anatolia), the Medes, Persians and Parthians (Iran) and the Bactrians (Afghanistan).

The Silk Route Name given to the overland trading route from China to Europe, which traversed the ancient territories of East and West Turkestan, Ariana, Bactria, Baluchistan, Persia and Anatolia on its westwards journey to the Maghrib with subsidiary routes branching off into India, Arabia and all the bordering countries to the north and south. No one knows exactly when the Silk Route first came into existence, but a combination of archaeological and historical evidence points to the existence of trade links between the Far East and the ancient kingdoms of Egypt, Phoenicia, Mesopotamia and Babylonia during the latter half of the 1st millennium BC and possibly much earlier. East Turkestan, especially in and around the Altai Mountains (which literally mean 'the mountains of gold'), has substantial deposits of gold, silver, copper and other precious and semi-precious metals and stones, as well as being the nearest source of jade to the Middle East and Europe. Consequently, the discovery of jade cylinders on archaeological sites in ancient Babylonia – coupled with evidence that Mesopotamian traders brought jade, as well as bronze, into Hungary and other parts of Europe – provide concrete evidence of trading links. Further evidence can be found in the journals of Marco Polo (the 13th-century Venetian explorer who traversed the Silk Route and served in the court of Kublai Khan), and also by the excavations of the Hungarian-born archaeologist, Sir Aurel Stein, in the Takla Makan Desert and Tarim Basin (East Turkestan), at the beginning of the 20th century.

Patterns of migration We can trace the great conquests and migrations that swept across Asia in all directions during the last 2,000 years

(from the Macedonian armies of Alexander the Great to the great empires of the Ottoman Turks), with each spreading different racial groups throughout the region, as well as bringing new ideas, skills, knowledge and beliefs. What is not so clear, however, is the exact pattern of smaller, less dramatic incursions and tribal movements that resulted from: attempts to escape invading armies, forced resettlement and the natural inclination to seek safer or more fertile environments. In addition, the existence of an established trade route always ensures a steady flow of people, ideas and skills accompanying the export of artefacts and raw materials.

Aryan migrations Occurred during the 2nd millennium BC, when Indo-European tribesmen migrated in successive waves from the Eurasian Steppes to the Indus and Nile Valleys. The majority settled in northern India, dominated the existing culture, established a caste system and later intermarried with the indigenous Dravidians. Initially, the Aryan invaders belonged to a number of separate tribal units and their inter-tribal rivalry and religious beliefs became the inspiration behind the Rig-Vedas (the earliest Hindu scriptures), which were integral in forming the basic tenets of Hinduism. The Aryans who migrated to Egypt and Syria founded the Hyksos Empire (c. 1720–1550 BC).

The Persian Empire Founded by Cyrus the Great in 549 BC when he united the Medes and the Persians (two small Iranian kingdoms) and went on to conquer Asia Minor and the Babylonian Empire. His grandson Darius (c. 522–486 BC) extended the empire northwards into Central Asia and eastwards as far as the Indus Valley.

Alexander the Great In 336 BC he inherited the throne of Macedonia and within thirteen years conquered all the Persian dominions, encouraging Greek colonization and cultural supremacy. After his death, in 323 BC, his empire was divided into three parts – the Macedonian (Greece), Ptolemaic (Egypt) and Seleucid (Iran).

The Parthian Empire (c. 250 BC–AD 229) Founded by Parthian and immigrant Scythian tribesmen who overthrew Alexander the Great's Greek-Macedonian successors and restored Persia (Iran) to local rule. It lasted for nearly 400 years despite ongoing conflicts with Rome.

The Roman Empire (*c.* 238 BC–AD 500) Reached its territorial peak at the beginning of the 2nd century AD, stretching from western Europe, through North Africa, Palestine, Turkey, the Caucasus and into western Mesopotamia, but continued to exist in some form until the end of the 5th century. In an attempt to make the empire easier to govern Diocletian (*c.* AD 284–305) divided it into western and eastern sectors and, in AD 306, Constantine (r. *c.* AD 306–338) built a Second Rome (Constantinople) on the site of ancient Byzantium, in Thrace (European Turkey), as an administrative centre for the eastern sector, which later became the Byzantine Empire.

The Sassanian Empire (*c.* AD 229–651) Founded by a powerful Persian family who led an uprising against the Parthians. Despite constant threats by Rome and the Byzantine Empire on its western border and incursions into its eastern territories by Huns and other Turkic tribes, Persia (Iran) emerged once more as a major political and cultural force.

The Byzantine Empire (*c.* 330–1453) Evolved from the eastern sector of the Roman Empire and – dating it from the founding of Constantinople, in 330, to the city's conquest by the Ottoman Turks, in 1453 – lasted, in some form, for over 1,000 years. The empire left a tremendous cultural and artistic legacy that has had a profound effect on the subsequent evolution of Russia, the Balkans and much of eastern Europe. During its existence, it acted as a Christian buffer against the spread of Islam from the East and brought Christian symbolism and attitudes into weaving.

The Caliphates and the Arab Empire (*c.* 632–*c.* 1492) Shortly after Mohammed's death, in *c.* 632, his followers elected a successor, Abu Bakr (*c.* 573–*c.* 634) and installed him as their spiritual and political leader (or Caliph) in their capital at Medina. Over the next 30 years, the Four Great Caliphs (Abu Bakr, Umar, Uthman and Ali) extended both Caliphate Islamic influence into Syria, Mesopotamia, Persia and Egypt. However, it was not until Mu'awiyah (*c.* 602–680) came to power, in 661, that these territories began to be united under central Caliphate control – with each region ruled through a general, a judge and a vizier (administrator). He made the position of Caliph hereditary, rather than elective, and his family (the Umayyads) ruled until AD 747, when the Abbasid family rebelled, established their capital in the newly built city of Baghdad (Syria), founded the independent Abbasid Caliphate and set in motion the disintegration of centralized control.

This process continued over the next 300 years, as a succession of rebellions by provincial generals established more breakaway Caliphates or empires. These included a faction of the Umayyads in southern Spain and the Berber Fatamids in North Africa, Egypt and Sicily. By the mid-10th century, the authority of the original Caliphate at Medina had practically disappeared and had been replaced by a loose confederation of independent states, unified by Islam and their adherence to Arab culture (even though, in some instances, the rulers were non-Arabs). During this period, the Arab Empire extended its political influence throughout North Africa, the Middle East and southern Europe, but invasions from the East during the 11th and 13th centuries by the Seljuk Turks and the Mongols, coupled with an ongoing conflict with the Crusaders in the West, saw Arab territory and influence gradually decline. The few remaining outposts of the Arab Empire finally collapsed during the 15th century when their Asian territory was overrun by the Ottoman Turks and their last stronghold in southern Europe disappeared with the fall of Granada, in Spain, in 1492. However, the Arab Empire spread Islam throughout much of Asia, made remarkable developments in literature, science, mathematics and astronomy, refined many arts and crafts (including weaving) and contributed to the migration of different ethnic groups throughout the region.

The Seljuk Empire (*c.* 1055–*c.* 1258) Founded by a sub-tribe of the Oghuz or Ghuzz branch of Turkic tribesmen. They derived their name from their former leader, Seljuk, who conquered Baghdad (the centre of the Arab Empire), in 1055, and ruled Persia, Iraq and most of Asia Minor. During the 12th century, their empire began to split into several independent states – the most influential of which were the Ayyubid dynasty in Egypt and Syria (founded by Kurds under Saladin) and the later Mameluke Empire in Egypt (founded by former Seljuk soldiers and mercenaries, including Kurds and Circassian slaves). The Seljuk Turks were Muslim converts who consolidated the influence of Islam, brought their weaving skills to the region and settled in large numbers throughout the Middle East.

The Mongol Empire (*c.* 1279–*c.* 1368) Can be traced to the rise of Timujin (*c.* 1162–*c.* 1227), who reunited the warring Mongol tribes and, in around 1206, was elected their leader under the title Genghis Khan ('Great Leader'). In 1220, he invaded Persia and, by 1279, the Golden Hordes (as his army became known) had conquered an area that stretched from the east coast of Asia to the Danube, and from China and the Siberian Steppes to the Arabian Sea. After Genghis Khan's death, the Mongol Empire devolved to his son, Chagatai, and eventually split between his two grandsons. In the eastern sector, Kublai Khan established the Yuan (Mongol) dynasty in China (*c.* 1279–1368). In the western sector, Hulagu captured Baghdad, in 1256, which he partly destroyed and then rebuilt, making it his winter residence and exercising his rule from Tabriz (Persia) during the summer months – stimulating the revival and later blossoming of Persian art and weaving. However, by the end of the 13th century, the invaders had been converted to Islam and a hundred years later most had been assimilated into the host cultures – bringing with them their own particular weaving traditions, skills and designs – thus allowing the countries in the Mongol Empire to revert to their former separate states.

The Ottoman Empire (*c.* 1290–*c.* 1923) Founded by another sub-tribe of the Oghuz or Ghuzz branch of Turkic tribesmen (*see* The Seljuk Empire, p. 54), who derived their name from their leader, Osman or Uthman (r. *c.* 1290–*c.* 1326). The Ottomans established an empire that at its height, in the 15th and 16th centuries, ruled an area stretching from the Zagros Mountains (in western Iran) through Turkey, Palestine, North Africa, the southern Caucasus and most of the Balkans into southwest Europe as far as Hungary. The Ottoman Empire was governed in accordance with Islamic law and non-Muslims (e.g., Greeks, Jews, Armenians), although allowed to practise their religions, were segregated, made to pay additional taxes, forbidden to carry arms, denied the privileges of full citizenship and suffered an annual levy of Christian youths who were forcibly converted to Islam and conscripted into the army.

The Ottoman Empire reached its political, cultural and artistic zenith during the 16th century under Suleiman the Magnificent (r. *c.* 1520–*c.* 1566), who ruled from Constantinople and showed a willingness to absorb European technology and employ highly skilled Albanian, Italian, Greek and other European slaves in government positions. His immediate successors, however, reversed his open policy and reverted to a form of Islamic isolationism that rejected anything western and employed only Islamic Turks in positions of authority. The result was a gradual decline in Ottoman fortunes and by the outbreak of the First World War, its boundaries were approximately those of modern Turkey, which became a republic and renounced its Caliphate (Islamic spiritual leadership) status in 1923/24. The Ottoman Empire had a profound effect on the evolution of weaving, partly through the natural spread of foreign skills and traditions throughout the empire and the enforced expulsions of indigenous ethnic groups (Armenians, Greeks, Kurds, etc.) and the mass settlement of ethnic Turks in Turkey and, to a lesser extent, the Balkans and elsewhere. (*See* Turks, Turkomen and the Turkic tribes, p. 49)

Tamerlane (*c.* 1336–*c.* 1405) The Mongol-Turkic Empire was revived briefly during the late 14th century by a descendant of Genghis Khan, known as Timur Lenk or Timur-the-Lame (anglicized to Tamerlane). He united Mongol and Turkic tribesmen and established an empire that stretched from his capital, Samarkand, in Central Asia, through Persia and Iraq to Syria and Egypt. After subjugating the western territories, he turned eastwards and marched on China, dying on route and bringing to an end four centuries of Mongol influence throughout the region.

The Persian Safavid dynasty (*c.* 1502–*c.* 1736) Founded by Ismail (r. *c.* 1500–*c.* 1524) and named after his ancestor Safi ad-Din. The Safavids unified Persia's Shiite Muslims and made Shia the state religion – bringing Persia into conflict with orthodox Sunnite Muslims in the Ottoman Empire. Under the Safavids, Persia achieved its peak of artistic and cultural expression, particularly in the field of rug and kilim weaving and during this period came to be seen in the West as the spiritual home of the oriental carpet. The Safavids, in general, and Shah Abbas (r. *c.* 1587–*c.* 1629), in particular, were responsible for moving a number of nomadic tribes (e.g., Afshar) to different parts of the country and also forming others into multi-ethnic political confederations (e.g., Shahsavan).

The Moghul Empire (*c.* 1526–*c.* 1857) Much of northern India had been under the control of Turkic Muslims from the 12th century. But it was not until a Mongol King of Afghanistan, Babur (*c.* 1483–1530), a descendant of Tamerlane, established the Moghul (a corruption of Mongol) Empire – stretching from Afghanistan to northern and central India – that Islam and Islamic culture began to have a profound effect on the development of Indo-Pakistani society. Forced conversion to Islam and the destruction of Hindu art and architecture led to religious conflict between Muslims and Hindus. Thus providing the stimulus for the Hindu reformer, Nanak (*c.* 1469–*c.* 1538), to develop Sikhism as a compromise between these two religious extremes. The ruling Moghuls (and their Turkic confederates) were heavily influenced by Persian culture and gradually incorporated aspects of Persian (and Arabic) arts, crafts and architecture (including weaving) into Indian artistic expression. This resulted in a fusion of styles that we now associate with the golden age of Indian art. The power of the Moghuls declined after the arrival of the British in the 18th century.

The Persian Qajar dynasty (*c.* 1794–*c.* 1906) Can be traced to Nadir Kuli (r. *c.* 1736–*c.* 1747), who successfully reclaimed Persian territory from Ottoman and Afghan invaders and laid the foundation for another leading Persian family, the Qajars, to establish a dynasty. The Qajars managed to maintain Persia's independence despite continuing pressure on its borders by the Ottoman and, later, the British and Russian Empires. A number of the kilims and rugs produced during this era (particularly those dating from the mid- to late 19th century) still appear on the market and they are considered by some dealers to be the last examples to contain the true spirit of Persian weaving.

The Persian Pahlavi dynasty (*c.* 1924–*c.* 1979) Founded by Reza Shah Pahlavi (r. 1925–41), after a period of rule by civil assembly following the decline of the Qajars. The Pahlavi dynasty (which takes its name from an ancient Perisan language) tried both to modernize the country (renaming it 'Iran' in 1936) and also to re-establish the golden age of Persian culture (achieved under the Safavids) by sponsoring traditional Persian arts and crafts, in particular the production of oriental rugs. Selected workshops in Isfahan, Quoom, Nain and other major cities were encouraged to produce finer and more sophisticated items, which in terms of technical perfection often surpassed the greatest Safavid carpets. However, some authorities believe that despite their superb craftsmanship most of these carpets lack the traditional Persian soul and should therefore be considered Iranian rather than Persian. In contrast, most kilims produced during the Pahlavi era still retain their traditional Persian character and appearance.

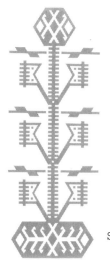

Stylized tree-of-life motif

Note: In the colour plates section the origin of each kilim is given in roman type. The origins of similar items are in *italic*. If the exact origin for an item is unknown, all possibilities are in roman. For a detailed explanation of the designs, *see* Chapter V.

1. **TRADITIONAL CAUCASIAN** *Soumak*: dragon design; *soumak* technique (regional, Nagorny Karabagh district, Azerbaijan SSR), 1875–1900

2. **SHAHSAVAN OF MOGAN** kilim: repeating all-over tree-of-life design; slitweave
(regional/tribal, Azerbaijan district, Iran), *c.* 1940

3. **ARMENIAN** ķilim: repeating medallion design; slitweave with supplementary weft wrapping
(regional, Armenia SSR), *c.* 1950

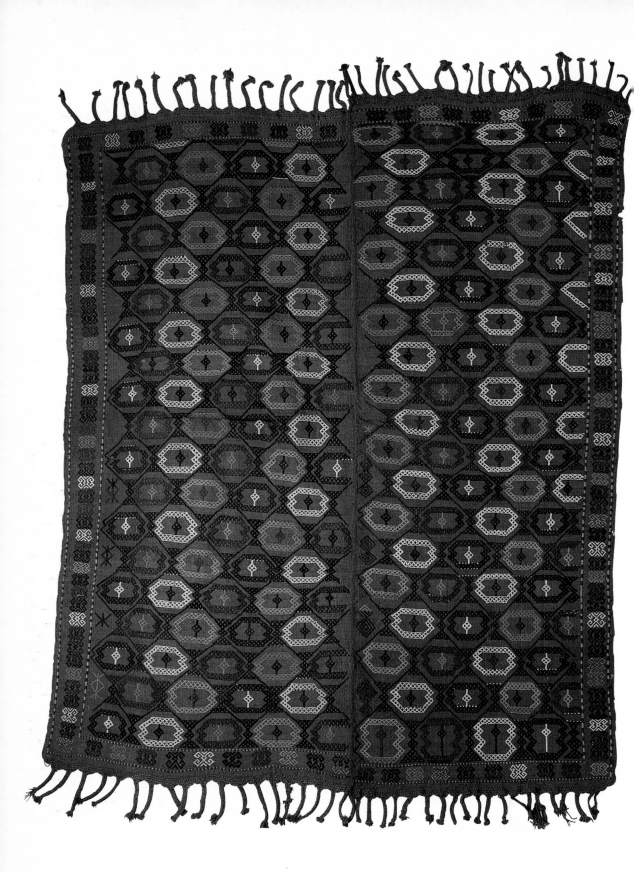

4. **EAST TURKISH** (Kars or Van) kilim: repeating geometric design; slitweave with supplementary weft insertion, woven in two halves (regional/tribal, Turkey/*Armenia*), 1920/30

5. **VAN** (Herki tribe) kilim: banded design; slitweave, woven in two halves (regional/tribal,
Turkey), contemporary

6. **ARDEBIL** kilim: repeating all-over geometric design; slitweave (regional/workshop, Iran),
contemporary

7. **AZROU** kilim: lattice design; plainweave with weft-faced patterning and insertion
(regional/tribal, Morocco), contemporary

8. **ROMANIAN BESSARABIAN** ('Gypsy') kilim: all-over floral design; slitweave (regional/tribal, Romania), contemporary

9. **TURKISH** (Ushak) kilim: repeating prayer arches with variant hand of Fatima, earring and leaf and vine motifs; slitweave (standard quality workshop, Turkey), contemporary

10. **TAIMANI AIMAQ** semi-pile kilim: panelled/compartmentalized pictorial design; slitweave
with supplementary pile sections (tribal, Afghanistan), contemporary

11. **BERGAMA** kilim: Scandinavian folk-art design; slitweave (superior quality workshop, Turkey), contemporary

12. **SOVIET CAUCASIAN** (Kazakh style) kilim: panelled/compartmentalized design with a central medallion on an open field; slitweave (workshop, USSR), contemporary (pre-independence)

13. **OUDZEM** kilim: banded design with a central panel/compartment; plainweave and weft-faced patterning (workshop, Morocco), contemporary

14. **BULGARIAN** kilim: repeating all-over stylized floral design; slitweave (workshop, Bulgaria), contemporary

15. **QASHGA'I** kilim: repeating scorpion/tarantula hexagons with supplementary star motifs; slitweave (tribal, Iran), 1940/50

16. **SHAHSAVAN** kilim: banded design; slitweave with supplementary weft twining (tribal, Iran), contemporary

17. **ZAIR** kilim: banded design with supplementary tassels; weft-faced patterning and plainweave with supplementary pile/tassel insertions (tribal, Morocco), contemporary

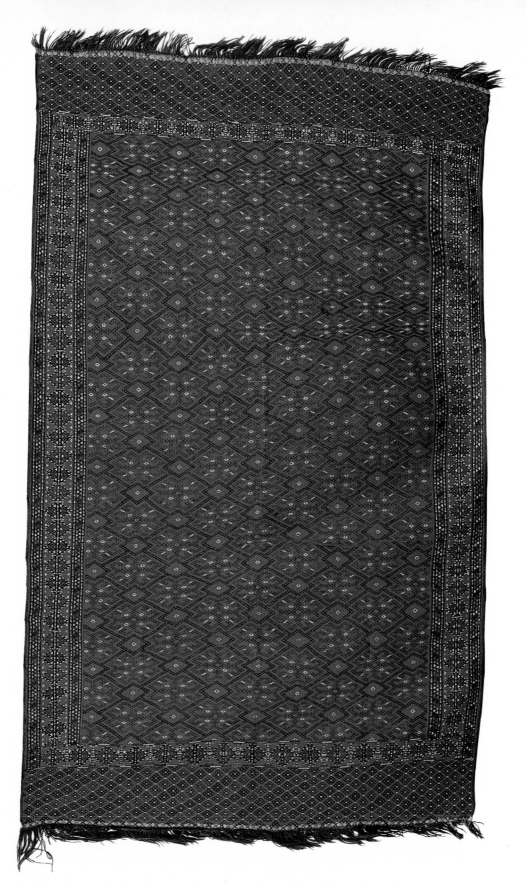

18. **YOMUT** kilim: lattice *gul* design; weft-faced patterning (regional/tribal, Afghanistan/*Uzbekistan*/*Turkmenistan*), contemporary

19. **BELOUCH** *dasterkan*: empty-field design; weft-faced patterning and weft wrapping (tribal, Iran/Afghanistan/*Pakistan*), contemporary

20. **YOMUT** *jallar*: lattice *gul* and floral design; weft-faced patterning (tribal, Afghanistan/Turkmenistan/*Uzbekistan*), contemporary

21. **SENNEH** kilim: skeletal medallion set against a variegated field of repeating all-over floral motifs; slitweave with weft inserts and curved wefts (regional/workshop, Iran), contemporary

22. **KERMAN AFSHAR** camel trapping: panelled design containing repeating floral, camel and bird motifs; double interlock, dovetailing and weft twining (tribal, Iran), contemporary

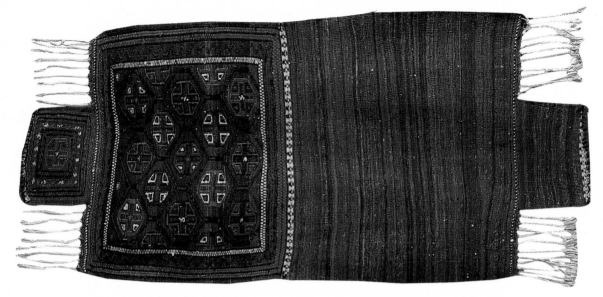

23. **KHUZETSTAN AFSHAR** *namakdan*: repeating cruxiform motifs on bag face, plainwoven reverse; double interlock, weft twining, weft-faced patterning and plainweave (tribal, Iran), contemporary

24. **KURDISH** *maffrash*: repeating all-over diamond motifs; weft wrapping, weft-faced patterning, double interlock and slitweave (tribal, north-west Iran), contemporary

25. NISHAPUR BELOUCH *soufreh*: triple cruxiform motifs, with stylized deer, bird and 'S' forms, set inside a sharply cuspidated field (indicating its special purpose); weft-faced patterning and weft wrapping (tribal, Iran/*Afghanistan*/*Pakistan*), contemporary

26. **BELOUCH** *malaki*: banded design; alternating rows of pile, weft-faced plainweave, weft wrapping and weft twining (tribal, Afghanistan/Pakistan/*Iran*), contemporary

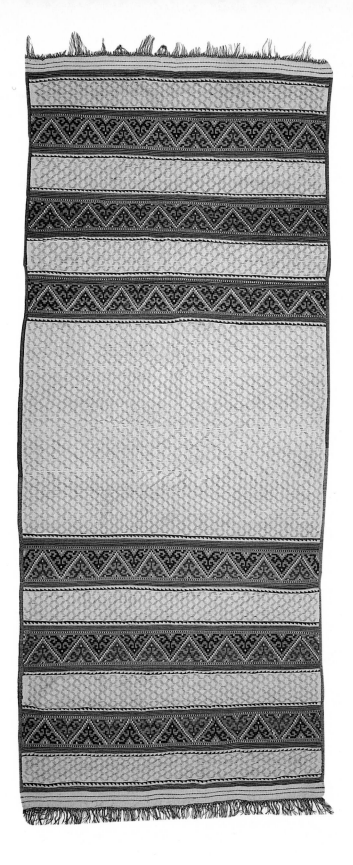

27. **SAR-I-PUL** (Tartari *safid*) kilim: banded design with empty field; weft-faced patterning and weft-faced plainweave (regional/tribal, Afghanistan), contemporary

28. **LURI** kilim: triple medallion design; slitweave (tribal, Iran), contemporary

29. **LABIJAR** kilim: medallion design; slitweave and double interlock (regional/tribal,
Afghanistan), contemporary

30. **VERAMIN** kilim: 'eye-dazzler' design; slitweave with contour bands (regional, Iran),
contemporary

31. **KONYA/AKSARAY** kilim: repeating all-over star and cruxiform design; slitweave (regional, Turkey), c. 1940

32. **KURDS OF KHORASSAN** kilim: repeating all-over star design; slitweave (tribal),
contemporary

33. **AFGHAN** 'refugee' kilim: repeating all-over diamond and cruxiform design; slitweave
(regional/tribal, Pakistan/*Afghanistan*), contemporary

34. **BIDJAR** kilim: medallion-and-corner design; slitweave (regional/tribal, Iran), contemporary

35. **SARKOY** kilim: floral and architectural design; slitweave and curvilinear weaving
(regional/workshop, Turkey/*Bulgaria*), contemporary

36. **QASHGA'I** kilim: panelled design; slitweave (tribal, Iran), contemporary

37. **OBRUK/ERZURUM** kilim: prayer rug with tree-of-life design; slitweave and supplementary weft wrapping (regional, Turkey), *c.* 1950/60

38. **FIRDOUS BELOUCH** *chanteh*: linear rows of repeating geometric motifs; weft-faced patterning and weft wrapping (regional/tribal, Khorassan Province, Iran), contemporary

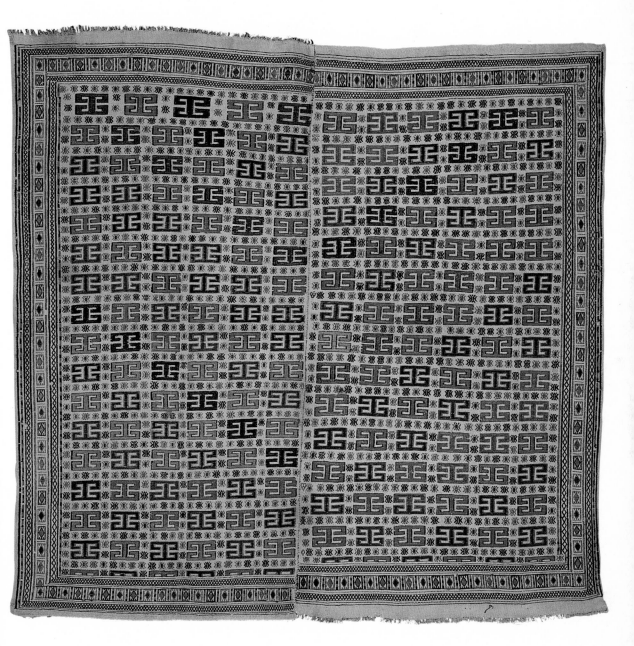

39. **TRADITIONAL CAUCASIAN** (Shirvan or Kuba) *verneh*: repeating all-over design; plainweave
with supplementary weft wrapping (regional, Azerbaijan/*Armenia*), 1920

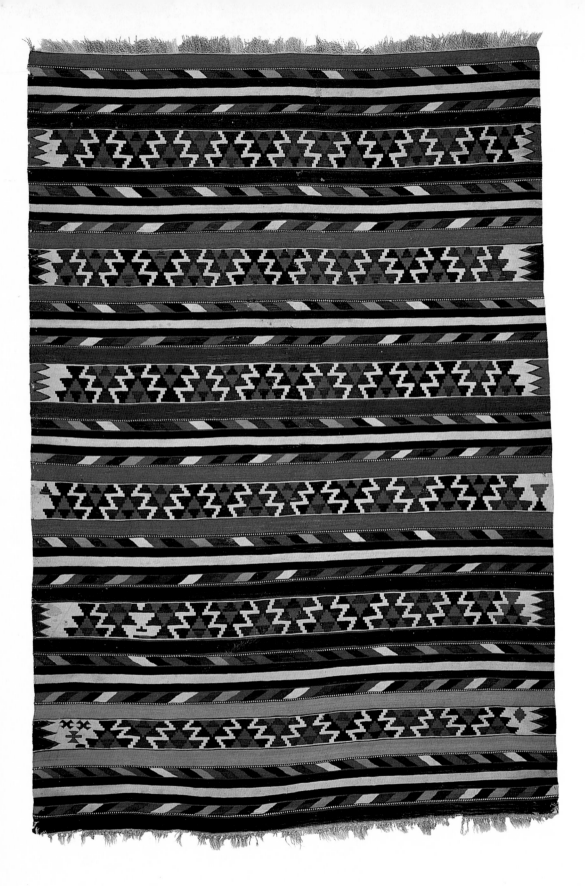

40. **SHIRVAN** kilim: banded design; slitweave (regional/tribal, Azerbaijan), *c.* 1900

41. **FARS** (Qashga'i, Luri, Khamseh) *jajim*: banded design; stripweave and warp-faced patterning
(tribal, Fars Province, Iran), *c.* 1925

42. **UZBEK** (Bokhara) waxed silk *ikat*: repeating all-over floral and stem design (tribal,
Uzbekistan/*Afghanistan*), *c.* 1850

CHAPTER V

Designs

Kilim designs are based on collective, rather than individual, expression – each weaving group has evolved a repertoire of designs based on their specific historical, cultural, religious and environmental experiences. Individual nuances may occur, but they are normally secondary to a faithful rendering of the weaving heritage of the tribe, village or region. The basic design repertoires of some weaving groups, mainly tribal, have hardly changed for centuries and the kilims they produce today still contain many of the time-honoured designs of their ancestors. However, kilim weavers also incorporate the events and experiences that have altered, and continue to modify, their way of life. This results in an on-going woven history that can be seen in the often subtle additions, omissions and alterations of individual motifs or design formats. For example, the sudden appearance of a new *gul* in kilims produced by a particular Turkoman tribe frequently corresponds to the conquest or assimilation of the tribe to whom the *gul* originally belonged. Similarly, the inclusion of tanks, helicopters and Kalashnikov assault rifles in Belouch and Taimani kilims can be traced to the Russian invasion of Afghanistan in 1979.

A basic understanding of kilim designs is important, not only in assisting identification, but also as a means of gaining a valuable insight into the history, culture and lifestyle of the weavers themselves.

Identifying kilims by their colour and design
Can be extremely difficult because a number of weaving groups from different parts of the kilim-weaving region produce items that are very similar in appearance. However, a kilim's design can eliminate some weaving groups or regions. For example, *gul* designs are almost exclusively produced in Central Asia and Afghanistan, so it is reasonably safe to assume that anything bearing this design did not originate from Turkey, Iran, North Africa, the Balkans or the Caucasus. Similarly, figurative designs are fairly common among tribal weavers in Iran and Afghanistan and are also found on some Balkan items, but they are extremely rare on Turkish or Central Asian kilims. Consequently, the first step in identification is to use the design as a means of reducing the possible options and then make further reductions by taking into account the colours and weaving techniques – some weaving groups, whose items employ very similar designs, use different colour schemes or weaving techniques. For example, both Zemmour (Moroccan) and Malatya (Turkish) kilims are produced in banded designs, but Zemmours are usually woven in plainweave and weft-faced patterning, with red grounds and fairly light secondary colours, whereas Malatyas employ slitweave, plainweave and supplementary weft-wrapping and have a much darker palette of browns, reds, blues, greens and black. (*See* Chapters II, VI and VII)

This process of elimination may not be sufficient to enable an exact attribution, but it should result in reducing a kilim's possible origins to a clearly defined geographical area or to a limited number of – often culturally or ethnically related – weaving groups.

The origins of kilim design

Kilim designs are drawn from a number of different religious, cultural and environmental sources and several common motifs and themes appear in items produced as far apart as Morocco and Afghanistan or the Balkans and Iran. However, it is extremely difficult, if not impossible, to say with absolute certainty how, when and where the majority of compositions and motifs evolved. Some are clearly rooted in specific religious symbolism (e.g., Islamic prayer-rug designs), but there are others (e.g., the tree of life) that possess a universal religious or spiritual resonance or may equally be merely secular renditions of a natural form.

The same is true of a number of motifs and design elements that have been drawn from nature (animals, flowers, etc.), the social environment (earrings, animal fetters, etc.) and abstract geometric patterns (swastikas, crosses, etc.). Many have an associated religious or mystical significance, but it is not always clear whether they are included because of their symbolism or simply because they enhance the overall composition.

Some motifs are still clearly recognizable as the plants, animals, birds or man-made objects (e.g. vines, camels, rifles, etc.) after which they are named. Others have become so abstract that there is no visible connection between their physical appearance and the objects that they are supposed to represent. It is often a matter of speculation as to whether the names relate directly to the object or whether they were established at a later date because a particular motif looked like, for example, an earring or a stepped mirror, when it was in fact derived from an entirely different source.

Names and symbolic interpretations Vary considerably from region to region, between different cultures and weaving groups, and among individual dealers and historians in the West. Consequently, a common motif such as a cross may be referred to by either its Western name or any one of its local names – e.g., *hac* (Turkish), *charkh palak* (Turkoman) or *salib* (Persian) – depending to a large degree on the individual dealer's affinity with specific weaving regions. For example, dealers who specialize in Turkish kilims will tend to use Turkish names and interpretations, and those who have a closer connection with Iran will generally employ a Persian (Farsi) equivalent.

Design limitations

Weaving techniques' effect on designs Closely connected because each individual kilim-weaving technique (e.g., plainweave, slitweave, etc.) is only capable of articulating certain types of designs. Consequently, weaving groups who use slitweave, for example, will tend to produce kilims with diagonal or stepped designs because the technical constraints of slitweaving make it almost impossible to produce striped or banded designs. (*See* Chapters II, VI and VII)

Geometric and curvilinear designs Most kilim-weaving techniques are more conducive to angular rather than curvilinear designs.

Consequently, the vast majority of compositions and motifs are either entirely geometric (swastikas, diamonds, etc.) or angular renditions of natural curvilinear forms (birds, animals, flowers, etc.). Some relatively curvilinear designs are produced, but these are normally confined to items from the more sophisticated regional and contemporary workshop groups and invariably employ some form of supplementary weaving (e.g., *soumak*, weft-wrapping or insertion techniques).

Figurative and non-figurative designs Both are found in kilims, but figurative motifs are extremely rare in items from certain regions. This is partly due to the intrinsic difficulty in making even highly stylized, angular interpretations of human or animal forms, using certain weaving techniques (*see* Chapter II), but is perhaps influenced more by tradition and the conflicting interpretations of the *Hadith*. For example, Sunnite Muslims, who are dominant in Turkey, North Africa, Afghanistan and Central Asia, generally forbid the depiction of human and animal forms (as idolatry), so consequently figurative motifs are rarely found on Turkish, North African or regional kilims from Afghanistan and the Central Asian Republics. However, a number of nomadic tribes (Belouch, Taimani, etc.), although officially Sunnite, ignore this convention and are among the most prolific producers of figurative kilims. Shiite Muslims, who form the majority in Iran, believe figurative expression to be perfectly compatible with the teachings of Islam and have, therefore, always produced items containing clearly discernible renditions of people, animals and birds. Similarly, the predominantly Christian regions of Armenia and the Balkans, although generally producing non-figurative items, are not bound by any iconoclastic constraints.

Although this theory of a predominantly religious division between figurative and non-figurative kilim producers is not universally accepted, the patterns of production generally conform to the respective concentrations of each religious group in different parts of the weaving region. However, the presence of minority religions and cultural groups in each kilim-weaving nation provide numerous exceptions to the rule. Purely commercial considerations have also begun to play an increasingly significant role, especially in the major contemporary workshop production centres and a number of items are now being made that are based on more naturalistic Western designs.

The anatomy of a rug

Spandrels (or corners) (A) Only found on kilims that have borders as part of their design. They are the four right-angled areas where the field meets the first or inner border.

Medallion (B) Any large central motif, usually spherical or diamond shaped, used as the focal point of the design.

Border (C) Runs around the inner perimeter of the kilim – they may be single or multiple, plain or contain internal motifs.

Field (D) The main area of the rug.

Ground Usually describes the underlying or background colour in any part of the kilim (e.g., a red ground medallion) – sometimes used as an alternative to 'field'.

Motif Any single form or cohesive combination of forms (e.g., a cluster of leaves), which is used as an element in the design.

Open field Either a totally undecorated monochrome field or one with only a few, widely spaced motifs.

Variegated field The same design covering different-coloured grounds – sometimes used in conjunction with a skeletal medallion.

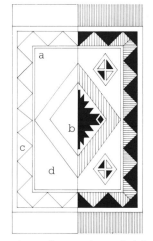

The anatomy of a rug: a) spandrels/corners, b) medallion, c) border, d) field

Palette (or dyer's palette) Term for the overall colour scheme (e.g., a sombre or pastel palette).

Patina The surface gloss or sheen of the kilim (e.g., a silky or dull patina).

All-over designs Any pattern that covers the entire field.

Repeating designs A single motif or group of motifs, which is repeated over the field.

Designs, motifs and symbolism

Basic compositions

Kilims are produced in a wide variety of designs, many of which can only be classified in the broadest visual terms, but there are a number of specific compositions that are used throughout the weaving region.

Pictorial designs (pls 10, 35, etc.) Employ a clearly defined scene drawn from nature, mythology or life rather than just containing naturalistic forms (e.g., garlands of flowers, human figures, etc.). The scene may be highly stylized or abstract, but is still recognizable as a landscape, portrait or a topical, historical or mythological event. Pictorial designs may be found in items from some regional and contemporary weaving groups, but are mainly in tribal kilims.

Afghan War designs Western term for a distinctive and highly collectable group of pictorial items that provide a contemporary woven record of the Russian invasion of Afghanistan as seen from the Afghan point of view. They

were produced by the Belouch, Taimani and some other Afghan nomadic tribes and feature tanks, helicopters, Kalashnikov rifles and a variety of other weapons and battle scenes. Authentic war rugs are confined to those produced during the conflict, but similar items are still being made in Afghanistan and Pakistan.

Presentation or ceremonial designs General term for a range of nomadic (mainly Belouch and Taimani) items that feature scenes from ceremonial occasions (e.g., a wedding or the visit of a tribal dignitary).

Animal designs (pls 22, 25, etc.) Feature fairly realistic representations of an animal or group of animals (usually lions or camels) and are mainly found in kilims from the Qashga'i, Luri, Shahsavan and other Iranian tribal groups.

Folk-art designs (pl 11, etc.) Generally based on European, particularly Balkan, and Armenian folk traditions. Found in some regional and contemporary workshop items from Armenia, the Balkans and Turkey.

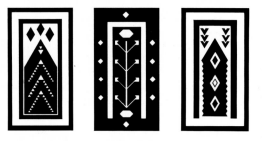

Prayer-rug designs. *From left*: diamond motifs; tree-of-life motif; repeating amulet/medallions

Prayer-rug designs (pl 37) Based on the physical structure of a mosque. Featuring the arch (*mihrab*) at the top of the composition where the sacred stone (*qibla*) is kept and which devotees face when praying. The lower part of the composition has a large rectangular area, known as the prayer field, representing the clean spot on which Muslims have to kneel during prayer. Prayer-rug compositions are commonly found in Turkish kilims (especially from Erzurum, Sivas, Keles and Obruk); Kurdish, Belouch and Taimani weavers also produce a number of items in this scheme.

Saph designs Sometimes referred to as multiple prayer rugs because they feature several adjacent prayer arches, running side by side, and are usually only found in kilims from Konya and a few other Turkish regional centres. A variation of the multiple arch scheme is also found as a border design in Karapinar and on a few other Turkish regional items.

Hatchli or enssi designs Traditionally appear on the kilims woven by Afghan and Central Asian nomads, which are used as door hangings (*enssis*) for their tents (*yurts*). *Hatchli* designs are variations on a central cross that divides the field into four quadrants, which are covered by a variety of tiny infill decorations and set within a complex border arrangement. The design has been ascribed various meanings including: a symbol of the security of the home; a husband and wife prayer rug; and a spiritual doorway to the Islamic heaven, with its four innermost gardens.

Tree-of-life designs (pl 37) Variations on the theme of a central trunk with branches extending on either side. It may be used in isolation or as a prayer-field decoration within a prayer-rug design. The tree of life itself is one of the oldest and most universal of all religious and mythological symbols – pre-dating all of the world's great religions and usually representing the

link between the human world and the worlds beyond. It is a common theme on Turkish (especially Sarkoy), Belouch and Taimani kilims and on items produced by some Iranian weaving groups.

The pomegranate design A variation of the tree-of-life scheme and is normally only seen in items from East Turkestan.

Gul designs (pls 18, 20) The basis of most Turkoman compositions – usually consisting of one or more types of lozenge-shaped motifs (or *guls*), repeated across the field in an 'all-over' format, culminating at the inner border. Some historians believe that the term *gul* is derived from a Persian word for 'flower'. Others trace its origins to an old Turkic word meaning 'clan' and point out that the Turkoman nomads have used *gul* motifs as tribal emblems or standards for centuries. Each tribe (Tekke, Yomut, Salor, Ersari, etc.) has its own unique variation and it was common practice for a conquered or assimilated tribe to have its *gul* adopted by the conquering tribe and then incorporated, usually as a subsidiary element, into their future compositions. *Gul* designs are found throughout Afghanistan and former Soviet Central Asia (Turkmenistan, Uzbekistan, etc.), but are rarely seen on kilims from other parts of the weaving region.

Ay-gul designs are more of an amulet/medallion or mandala than a standard Turkoman *gul* and are believed to symbolize eternity or possibly the moon. They are used in some East Turkestan kilims.

Medallion-and-corner designs (pls 21, 34) Consist of a central medallion, set against either an open or a decorated field, contained within a border that echoes to varying degrees the form of the medallion in its four corners. The size, shape and contours of the medallion and corners vary considerably, but they are all believed to represent a worm's eye view of the inside of a mosque dome (i.e., the medallion

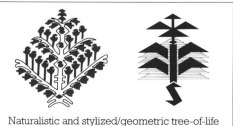

Naturalistic and stylized/geometric tree-of-life motifs. Taken from Caucasian kilims

mirrors the central boss and the corners represent the perimeter of the dome). It is sometimes referred to as the 'book-cover' design because it was traditionally used as a decoration on the tooled leather covers of the Koran. Medallion-and-corner designs are much less common in kilims than pile rugs, but are still found in some items from various weaving regions – with the possible exception of the former Soviet Central Asian Republics. They range in style from the relatively curvilinear designs produced by some of the more sophisticated regional and contemporary weaving groups to the bold angularity of many nomadic and tribal items.

Amulet/medallion designs (pls 1, 3, etc.) Stem from some ancient tribal emblem or identifying standard, rather than Islamic symbolism. They may have originally been derived from an environmental source (i.e., a bird, animal or plant used as a heraldic symbol in the same way as the Russian bear, the French lion or New Zealander fern with perhaps subtle variations like the German eagle, the Polish white eagle and the bald eagle in America). Some amulet/medallions are closely associated with specific origins (e.g., dragons, eagles, etc.) and are consequently referred to in the trade as, for example, 'Dragon Soumaks' or 'Eagle Kazakhs'. However, it is unclear whether these associations are based on historical reality or whether someone simply decided that a certain design resembled a dragon or eagle and the association has stuck. Amulet/medallion designs are found in kilims throughout the entire weaving region, but are especially common in Caucasian, nomadic and tribal/regional weaving groups in Turkey and Iran.

Pole medallions Have two or more medallions connected by a central pole or rod. They are found in the same range of kilims as other amulet/medallions.

European designs (pls 8, 11, 35) Influence the kilims made by a number of weaving groups, mainly in the Balkans, Turkey and China. Some are based on traditional folk-art designs (pl 11) and others on the bold, opulent floral schemes pioneered, during the 17th and 18th centuries, by the Aubusson and Savonnerie workshops in France and later found in a simplified form in 19th-century Caucasian kilims. European designs are now employed on some contemporary kilims produced in North Africa, Turkey and China. (*See* Sarkoy, p. 140)

Turkish Karabaghs – based on the old Caucasian kilims from the Karabagh region – are now produced, mainly around Erzurum, and are usually marketed as Turkish Karabaghs or simply Karabaghs. Their designs vary, but are based on large floral bouquets set against an open or sparsely decorated field.

Bessarabian kilims (pl 8) originated in Romania and are distinguished from Karabaghs by their use of symmetrical rows of stylized flowers set against a black or blue-black field. These designs are also now common on Chinese contemporary workshop kilims, which may be marketed as Chinese Bessarabians or simply Chinese kilims and also some Turkish Karabaghs, which may be marketed as either Karabaghs or Bessarabians.

Art deco and other modern Western designs can also be found on some contemporary workshop kilims, mainly from China, Turkey and, to a lesser extent, the Balkans.

Floral designs (pls 21, 42, etc.) Employ a variety of leaf, frond or floral motifs – either in all-over or repeating schemes, or set against an open or sparsely decorated field – as the predominant compositional feature. Floral motifs are frequently used in conjunction with medallion-and-corner, tree-of-life and other standard formats and there may be some debate whether, for example, these are primarily floral designs set inside a medallion-and-corner format or medallion-and-corner designs employing floral elements. They are found on a wide range of items from Turkey, Iran and the Balkans.

All-over and repeating floral formats (pls 2, 8, etc.) Usually found on Bessarabian and some Karabagh kilims and also on a number of items from Turkey (Sarkoy and Reyhanli, etc.), Iran (Senneh, Bidjar and Shahsavan, etc.), the Balkans and China.

Repeating floral motifs (pl 22, etc.) Sometimes used – often in a highly abstract form – by Belouch and Kirghiz weavers and also occasionally on items produced throughout the former Soviet Central Asian Republics and East Turkestan. (*See Boteh* designs)

Simple floral formats (pl 35, etc.) Employ large floral bouquets on open or sparsely decorated fields. (*See* European designs)

Boteh designs Derived from a Persian word meaning 'cluster of flowers' – known in the

West as the 'Paisley design' (after the town in Scotland associated with introducing this motif into Western textile production). The exact origins of the *boteh* motif are obscure – some experts have traced them to Kashmir, in India, others to Iran. It has been seen as representing such diverse objects as a leaf, a pine-cone, a foetus, a male sperm and the Zoroastrian flame. It is most commonly found in an all-over repeating format that became closely associated with the town of Mal-e-Mir, in the Serabend district of west central Iran, and is sometimes referred to as the *mir-i-boteh*. The size and articulation of individual *botehs* vary considerably. They are most commonly found on Iranian kilims, especially from Senneh, but may sometimes be used by weavers from other parts of the weaving region.

Herati designs Derived from the town of Herat (now in Afghanistan) which, when part of the Persian Empire, produced items in this design. Composed of a central floral head contained within a diamond-shaped framework with four outwardly curling crescent motifs on each side, it is frequently referred to as the *mahi* or fish-in-the-pond design because some authorities trace its origins to Persian mythology, which held that the world was supported by four swimming fish. It is mainly found on Iranian kilims, especially those produced around the towns of Ferahan (an alternative name for the design) and Hamadan, as well as the provinces of Azerbaijan, Kurdistan and Khorassan.

Panelled designs (pl 36, etc.) Divide the field into panels or segments usually containing alternating motifs or simply different-coloured grounds. They are especially common in Qashga'i kilims, but are sometimes found in Bakhtiari, Luri and occasionally Kazakh, Kirghiz and other Central Asian as well as North African items.

Lattice designs (pl 7, etc.) Less clearly differentiated variations of panelled designs, in which the infill motifs and ground colours are sometimes the same in adjacent panels. Commonly found on Belouch, Central Asian and some North African kilims.

Compartmental designs (pl 13, etc.) Similar to panelled designs, but based on one or more central compartments (or panels) set within a banded or all-over format. Employed mainly in Moroccan and other North African items and occasionally in items from elsewhere.

Striped and banded designs (pls 26, 40, etc.) Feature vertical (striped) or horizontal (banded) rows of different-coloured segments, with or without infill decorations, across the length or breadth of the kilim.

Striped designs are normally found only on stripwoven kilims (e.g., *jajims* or *ghudjeri*) which are produced occasionally by Turkoman, Qashga'i, Luri and a few other tribal weaving groups.

Banded designs can be produced by a wide variety of weaving techniques; they are the dominant format throughout North Africa and are commonly found in items from weaving groups throughout the entire weaving region, especially Turkey, Afghanistan and Iran.

Dragon designs (pl 1) Not realistic portrayals of dragons, as in Chinese or Tibetan rugs, but highly stylized forms that may or may not be based on actual dragon motifs. The two major variations are both derived from 19th-century Caucasian kilims and are usually either large heraldic motifs or schemes based on angular interpretations of the letter 'S' that are now seen as forming a specific and highly collectable sub-group referred to as Sileh kilims. Modern versions of these designs are sometimes produced by contemporary weaving groups, mainly in Turkey, Iran and the former Soviet Caucasian Republics. (*See* Dragon motifs, p. 103)

Religious motifs

Most of the purely religious motifs found on kilims are based on Islamic symbolism. However, Christianity, Buddhism, Hinduism and Zoroastrianism, as well as ancient animistic cults, have also played a part in creating the repertoire of motifs used in kilim designs. It is sometimes unclear which, if any, of the religious sources is most closely associated with certain motifs. For example, the swastika, tree of life and cross recur in a number of religious mythologies and, although their individual meanings may vary in accordance with specific dogmas, they should be treated as universal rather than specific religious symbols. Similarly, the specific religious connection of the *boteh* motif, for instance, depends entirely on which of its several possible origins you choose to accept. It must also be remembered that interpretations of the same motif may vary, not only between different religions, but also within the various sects or factions of the same religious group. (*See* Chapter IV)

Islamic motifs Usually connected to either the physical structure of a mosque (e.g., *mihrab* or prayer arch), the objects associated with worship (e.g., washing vessel) or the Islamic after-life (e.g., garden/paradise). Quotations from the Koran (that have sometimes become totally abstracted) are also occasionally found in kilim designs. (*See* Prayer-rug designs, p. 100, *Saph* designs, p. 100, *Hatchli* or *enssi* designs, p. 100, and Medallion-and-corner designs, p. 100). The following are Islamic motifs. Washing vessel: used to purify oneself before prayer. Hanging lamp or incense burner: used in a mosque. The hand of Fatima: usually depicted as a splayed right hand ('the hand of honour' as opposed to the left hand, 'the hand of dis-honour'). It is one of the most profound of all Islamic symbols. The thumb is said to represent the Prophet Mohammed; the first finger, Fatima (his daughter), who is also known as the 'weaver'; the second finger, Ali (her husband); the third and fourth, their sons (Hasan and Hussain). It is also used to symbolize the five pillars (or fundamental duties) of Islam and, as such, the very basis of religious belief. However, the open hand as a symbol of power and protection from the evil eye pre-dates Islam and has also been used as a means of divination by a number of Islamic, Hebrew, Christian and other occult practitioners and movements.

Universal motifs These appear in the mythology and symbolism of a number of major religions and can sometimes be traced to the earliest animistic cults. Specific interpretations may differ slightly between religions, but they are usually variations of the same general theme. However, it is not always clear whether they are now being used symbolically or simply as pictorial objects taken from the weaver's mythology or physical environment. (*See* Tree-of-life designs, p. 100)

Pomegranates symbolize fertility, due to the numerous seeds contained in its fruit, and were used as design motifs in Central Asia before being brought into China before the 1st century BC. It is a common motif on old East Turkestan and contemporary Sinkiang rugs, particularly as part of an overall tree-of-life scheme.

Dragons appear in various forms – each with its own distinctive range of powers, attributes and associations – in cultures and places as diverse as China, Polynesia, Ancient Egypt, Celtic Britain and the Aztec and Inca civilizations of South and Central America. Dragons are essentially a fusion of the snake god and the bird god (the *nagas* and *garudas* of Hindu/Buddhist mythology), adapted to suit local conditions and survival demands – often taking on some of the physical and mystical attributes of other native deities. For example, in maritime cultures, dragons are frequently depicted as fish and, in Celtic and Icelandic legends, the salmon was not only believed to be a manifestation of a dragon, but it was also thought that it could magically transform humans. The Celtic hero, Finn or Fionn, immediately became a seer after eating the 'Salmon of Knowledge'. In contrast, in desert kingdoms – such as Ancient Babylon (modern-day Iraq) – the dragon adopted the form and qualities of a lion, merging with those of an eagle and a snake, in order to guard Ishtar Gate at the threshold of the most sacred part of the city. This role of dragons as guardians or protectors is a recurring theme throughout the entire weaving region. They are variously regarded as the 'masters of wind and water', the 'keepers of the tree of life' and the 'custodians of the secrets of the universe'. They are also considered to be symbols of fertility and protectors from the evil eye and are found on kilims from various parts of the weaving region, although they are perhaps most closely associated with old Caucasian (especially Vishapogorg) items. Also known as *ejders* or *ejdehahs*. (*See* Dragon designs, p. 102)

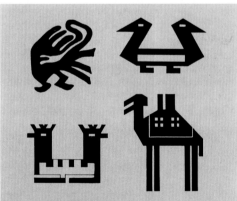

Animal motifs. *From top left clockwise*: dragon or *ejder* motif; double-headed bird/peacock motif; fabulous beast/bird motif; camel motif

Lions are universal symbols of strength and valour, and are traditionally employed as protectors or guardians – warding off both physical and supernatural threats. Lions are most commonly found in Belouch and Iranian (especially Qashga'i and Luri) tribal kilims. Also known as *sheers*.

Horses are the symbolic messengers of numerous cultures and appear primarily on tribal items – mainly from Iran, Afghanistan and Central Asia.

Camels are found on numerous, mainly tribal items, predominantly throughout Iran, Afghanistan and North Africa. There are several references in the Koran to a she-camel being sent as a messenger or as a test from Allah. Also known as *shotors*.

Birds are universal symbols of messages and portents and, in many religions, the carriers of dead souls from one world to the next. They are found in both realistic and in highly abstracted forms throughout the entire weaving region. Also known as *kus*, *gush*, *gonjishk* or *garudas*. (*See* Animal designs, p. 99)

Peacocks are closely associated with ancient Persia – where the rulers sat upon the peacock throne – and feature strongly in Persian mythology, culture and art. The peacock is also the national bird of India and the Hindu Rig-Vedas make several references to peacocks as 'bringers of rains', 'killers of serpents' and 'steeds of the gods'. Chinese, Japanese and other religious and mythological systems throughout Asia variously associate peacocks with courage, beauty, pride, lamentation and the Devil (referred to as the Peacock Angel by the Yezidis of northern Iraq). There is also a widespread belief that peacock feathers have the power to ward off malevolent forces – probably because their markings resemble dozens of protective eyes – and that different parts of the bird can provide antidotes for everything from poison, tuberculosis, paralysis, asthma, headaches and catarrh to impotence and barrenness. Not surprisingly

Star motifs. *From top left clockwise*: eight-pointed star; cruxiform star and cross; star/diamond

Stylized bird or *kus* motifs

peacocks are common motifs on kilims throughout the entire weaving region, with the exception of North Africa, and are depicted with either one or two heads. Also known as *tahwus*.

Snakes are universal symbols of strength and fertility and may be considered either good or evil, depending on each individual religion's attitude towards sex and sexual imagery. In Islamic cultures, snakes do not have the same association with lust and temptation that they do in Christianity – consequently, they are generally considered to be powerful and benign talismans, ensuring both personal and agricultural fecundity and protection from evil influences. Also known as *yilans*, *mars* or *nagas*.

Stars are found on kilims throughout the entire weaving region. The symbol is generally interpreted as signifying spiritual and corporeal happiness, although this meaning can only truly be applied to six-sided stars. Different symbolic meanings should be applied to four-pointed stars (stability, wholeness and the mysteries of nature), five-pointed stars (good luck, protection and power over matter), seven-pointed stars (perfection), eight-pointed stars (wisdom) and nine-pointed stars (the spiritual exaltation of man and matter). Also known as *setarehs* or *yildiz/yulduz*.

Crosses are arguably the oldest amulet or symbolic talisman in the world, pre-dating Christianity by at least 3,000 years. The symbol is found in slightly different forms in cultures as far apart as the Middle Eastern Kassite (*c.* 2nd millennium BC) and Assyrian (*c.* 1st millennium BC) kingdoms, Celtic Britain and pre-Christian Europe, China and pre-Columbian America. Specific meanings vary from culture to culture, but there are a number of common themes, including, protection from evil, power over corporeal existence and as a symbol of the physical world. Also known as *salib*, *charkh palak*, *hac* or *sogdian*.

Swastikas and sauvastikas are universal religious and magical symbols – found in cultures throughout Asia, Europe and America – and are used in kilims produced throughout the entire weaving region. The swastika derives its name from a fusion of two Sanskrit (ancient Indian) words for 'well being' and 'good fortune' and has been ascribed several meanings, including, happiness, the heart of Buddha and the number ten thousand. It was a symbol of the Supreme God among early Aryan civilizations and came to signify the sun in India and China and was adopted by followers of the Jain religion (which arose out of Hinduism and Buddhism). The true swastika has its short arms facing to the right, which signifies an anticlockwise rotation, so following the daily motion of the sun – from East to West, with the light – is often interpreted as a symbol of *karma* or the cycle of life.

The sauvastika is a mirror image of the swastika (i.e., the short arms face to the left), indicating a clockwise rotation, which moves against the daily motion of the sun, away from the light. In Hinduism, the swastika and the sauvastika represent the male and female principles, good and evil, light and dark, as manifest in the god Ganesh (lord of knowledge and learning) and the goddess Kali (devourer of the souls of the dead and guardian of dark or forbidden knowledge).

Magical motifs Most religious symbols are believed to have some magical properties, in that they afford general inspiration and protection to the believer, but there are a number of motifs commonly used in kilims that can be considered magical talismen. Such motifs are aimed specifically at warding off evil influences or bestowing good fortune, on both individuals and the tribe.

Scorpion/tarantulas are usually highly stylized variations on the pattern of several hooked legs extruding from a diamond-shaped body and are believed to be a charm against venom or poison. Also known as *akrep* or *sary ichyan*.

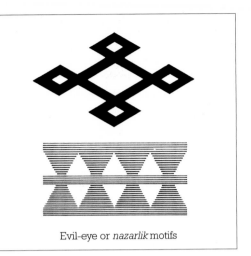

Evil-eye or *nazarlik* motifs

Wolf's mouth/track is a protective motif against attack from wolves and other predators. Also known as *kurt agzi/izi*.

Evil-eye protection is found in many forms, both as separate motifs or as individual motifs and as border designs – and known by as many different names – throughout the entire weaving region. There is a widespread belief that a 'look' can bring mischief and misfortune and that the best way to counter the evil eye is to show a stronger eye to potential enemies. Consequently, most evil-eye motifs are diamond- or lozenge-shaped, emulating the human eye. Also known as *nazarlik* or *goz*.

Elibelinde are fertility symbols that take the form of a woman (or goddess), often pregnant. They may be fairly realistic or highly abstracted and are sometimes referred to as the 'hand-on-hips motif' because the central feature resembles the line of someone's shoulders with their arms akimbo.

Hooks are very similar to the 'S' motif believed to symbolize the dragon, but are also shown as a mirror image (i.e., the short arms of the 'S' pointing to the left – 'Z' – rather than to the right). The hook's exact derivation and meaning are obscure – it may be a variation of the swastika/sauvastika – but it is generally believed to protect against the evil eye. Also known as *cengel* or *alaja*.

Hook or *cengel* and 'S' motifs

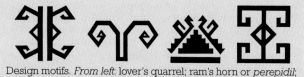

Design motifs. *From left*: lover's quarrel; ram's horn or *perepidil*; pair of birds; camel's neck or *sainah*

Ram's horn motifs are depicted in various ways on kilims from different parts of the weaving region and, although there are slight differences in emphasis. They are generally symbolic of power, virility and masculine virtues. The motif is known by many names, including, *perepedil*, *kochboynuzu*, *kuchkor*, *gocnak buynuz* and *muiiz*.

Heraldic motifs Some motifs are used specifically as tribal insignia and, although they often have an additional protective (or talisman) function, their main purpose is to identify and mark anything owned by or produced by the tribe. (*See Gul* designs, p. 100, and Amulet/medallion designs, p. 101)

Wasms are tribal insignia used by weavers throughout North Africa. They vary considerably in size and shape and, although not always clearly discernible as individual motifs, often provide the underlying design element for a number of basic compositions. The word *wasm* means brand or distinguishing mark in Arabic, and nomadic tribes have traditionally used their individual *wasms* to identify their animals and possessions. It was also common for women to be tattooed or branded on their faces, necks, hands or feet, with the tribal *wasm*, although this practice is in decline.

Geometric motifs A number of geometric motifs, which cannot be traced directly to either religious-magical symbols or natural forms, are also used in kilim designs.

Frets or lattices are general terms for a variety of linear, inter-locking motifs – usually employed as border patterns – derived from the old Anglo-Saxon word 'fretan'

(meaning 'to eat away'). All these motifs have the appearance of angular furrows or mazes, as seen from above. They are known by a variety of names in different parts of the weaving region, including, *chetanik* (Turkoman), *kerege nuska* (Kirghiz) and *wan* (Chinese).

Meanders are any sinuous, undulating linear motifs – normally used as border designs – that are generally based on either the meandering course of a river, or stream, or on the labyrinthine growth pattern of tendrils, or vines. They often incorporate additional motifs (leaves, etc.) and, depending on the region and additional motifs, are known by different names, including, *su yolu* in Turkish (meaning 'running water') and *iashil su* in Turkoman (meaning 'green water'), which are generally believed to symbolize vitality and life.

Environmental and lifestyle motifs A wide variety of motifs are drawn directly from the weaver's physical environment and lifestyle and have been incorporated – in realistic or highly stylized versions – into kilim designs throughout the entire weaving region. Some of these motifs have a clear religious or magical symbolism, but many have either no discernible meaning or only a vague and often disputed suggestion of symbolic intent.

Environmental motifs include running water, trees, vines, clouds, floral and vegetal forms, and the tracks and bodily parts of animals. For example, *gapyrga* (ribs), *buynuz* (horns), *it taman* (trace of the dog motif), *dyrnyk* (claws), *ok gozi* (arrow point), *chakmak* (lightning), *umurtka* (vertebrae motif), *uriik gul* (apricot blossom), *ovadan* (floral form known as the flourishing or beautiful motif) and the *ay kochot* (moon motif).

Lifestyle motifs include people, domestic animals, jewelry and personal possessions. For example, *insan, mard, zan* (human figures); *dast, el, gelin barmak* (hand); *tarak, shooneh* (comb); *kupe, sarkhalka* (earrings); *chemce* (spoon) and *sacbagi* (hairband).

Magical and lifestyle motifs. *From left*: earring or *kupe*; fertility or *elibelinde*; animal fetter or *bukagi*

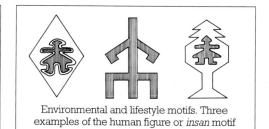

Environmental and lifestyle motifs. Three examples of the human figure or *insan* motif

CHAPTER VI

The weaving nations, territories and regions

Some contemporary weaving nations now occupy territory that was known historically by a different name (e.g., Iran was called Persia and Turkey, Anatolia). Others have been formed by the amalgamation of smaller, independent territories or states (e.g., Afghanistan from Ariana, Bactria and parts of ethnic Baluchistan); or, alternatively, partitioned from a larger, traditionally homogeneous, region (e.g., Turkmenistan from Turkestan).

Consequently, the exact geographical, ethnic and cultural relationship between the 'old' and 'new' territories can be extremely confusing, especially as there is often a lack of consistency, not only in the names used by individual dealers and historians, but also in the exact territorial divisions to which the name refers. For example, many dealers still market all Turkish kilims as Anatolian, despite the fact that the country has been called Turkey since 1923 and that Anatolia was only ever the eastern (Asian) part of the region. Similarly, items produced in the former Soviet Caucasian Republics are still often referred to collectively as Caucasian, even though the region is now comprised of a number of independent republics and Caucasian kilims, as a homogeneous general weaving group, have not been produced since the early part of this century. In addition, the dissolution of the Soviet Union, in 1991, negates the way Caucasian and Central Asian kilims have been classified for the last 50 years.

To minimize any possible confusion a basic understanding must be developed of the geographical and cultural relationship between the 'old' and 'new' weaving territories and nations, as well as the division between items that are produced by 'historical' and 'contemporary' weaving groups from the same region.

The ancient weaving nations, territories and regions

Anatolia Traditional name given to the Asian part of Turkey, which begins on the eastern side of the Bosporus Straits. It is possibly derived from an alternative name for the region, Andolu, a compound of two Turkish words, *ana* (mother) and *dolu* (full), which implies the concept of a pregnant mother or fecund earth. At the height of the Ottoman Empire, Anatolian suzerainty extended into Europe as far as Hungary and the Balkans and covered much of North Africa, the Middle East, parts of Iran and the Caucasus. It is still common practice for dealers to refer to Turkey as Anatolia and describe modern Turkish kilims, particularly those of village or tribal origin, as Anatolian. (*See* Turkey, p. 113)

Ariana Ancient name for part of Afghanistan.

Armenia (Ancient or Ethnic) Centred on a region in the Caucasus that was once the centre of the ancient Urartu civilization and was later occupied by ethnic Armenians during the 1st millennium BC. They founded a culture that, at its height, rivalled the power and influence of the Roman Empire and controlled a territory that covered most of the Caucasus and a significant part of Asia Minor and the Middle East. During the last 2,000 years the territory has been invaded, conquered, divided, annexed and partially reunited, before being conquered and divided again by a succession of invading armies: the Macedonians of Alexander the Great (331 BC), the Roman Empire (2nd century BC), the Byzantine Empire (4th century AD), the Arabs (7th century AD), the Seljuk Turks (11th century AD), the Mongols (13th century AD) and from the 16th century until its incorporation into the Soviet Union, in 1922, it was caught between the rival ambitions of the Persians and the Ottoman Turks. Ethnic Armenians now live in the Armenian Republic and, to a lesser extent, other former Soviet Republics, as well as other countries in the Middle East and Asia Minor. (*See* Armenians, p. 48)

Bactria Ancient name for an area in Afghanistan. Famous for giving its name to the Bactrian breed of camels.

The Balkans The most eastern of Europe's three southern peninsulas, deriving its name from the Balkan Mountains in Bulgaria, bounded by the Adriatic and Ionian Seas to the west and the Aegean, Mamara and Black Seas to the east. The countries generally considered to be part of the Balkans are Greece, Bulgaria, Albania, Yugoslavia, Romania and the European part of Turkey (Thrace). During the Ottoman Empire much of the Balkans was under Turkish rule and the flatweaving traditions of the region were greatly influenced by kilims from the East. Today, only Romania, Bulgaria, European Turkey and to a lesser extent Albania are significant producers of kilims for the Western market. (*See* Albania, p. 120, Bulgaria, p. 110, and Romania, p. 112)

Baluchistan (Ethnic) Name given to the traditional territory of the Belouch or Baluchi nomads, which extended from Pakistan into Afghanistan and eastern Iran, and is now the name of provinces in south-west Pakistan and east Iran. There is an old saying that Allah made Baluchistan from the areas that nobody else wanted and it is probably the forbidding nature of the terrain that has enabled the Belouch, and the other tribal groups in the region, to retain their traditional way of life. Some kilims are still made in the Province of Baluchistan, but the majority of Belouch weavings are produced in their traditional territories in Afghanistan and Iran and, since the Afghan-Russian War, Pakistan. (*See* Belouch, p. 124)

Barbary Ancient name for the Maghrib region of North Africa derived from the original inhabitants (the Barbari or Berbers) and made famous by tales of the Barbary Coast and by the pirates who plied their trade from the 16th to the 19th centuries. It is now divided between Morocco, Tunisia, Algeria and part of Libya.

Byzantium Ancient city in the European part of Turkey (Thrace) and the site of Constantinople (founded as a Christian city, in AD 330, by the Roman Emperor, Constantine), which became the administrative centre of the eastern half of the Christian Roman Empire. It gave its name to both the Byzantine Empire and to the fusion of Western and Eastern art and architecture that came to be known as Byzantine Art. It is now the site of Istanbul.

The Caucasus Traditional kilim-weaving region lying north and south of the Caucasian Mountains, bounded by the Black Sea to the west and the Caspian Sea to the east, and bordering Turkey and Iran to the south. For much of the last 2,000 years, the region has been subjected to a succession of invasions – by Mongols, Turkomen, Persians, Ottoman Turks, Russians and other racial groups – and different parts of the region were periodically under the control of one or more of their powerful neighbours. Not surprisingly, the Caucasus now arguably has the most varied and complex racial, cultural and religious mix in the kilim-producing world, with around 350 different tribal groupings who speak over 90 languages and dialects. The region to the north of the Caucasian Mountains is known as the Cis-Caucasus and the region to the south as the Trans-Caucasus. The Caucasus were incorporated into the Soviet Union during the early part of the 20th century – forming the Armenian, Azerbaijan and Georgian SSRs (which became independent states on the dissolution of the Soviet Union in 1991) and the Daghestan ASSR. (*See* The former Soviet Caucasian Republics and Traditional Caucasian kilims, p. 115)

East Turkestan Eastern territories of the Turkomen originally known as Kashgaria (after the town of Kashgar) and now the Sinkiang (or Xinjiang Uygur) Autonomous Region of China. East Turkestan centres on the vast arid desert and semi-desert of the Tarim Basin and is bounded by Mongolia to the north, Tibet to the south, the former Soviet Union to the west and China to the east. It is the only part of modern China that has not been extensively settled by the Han Chinese and is still largely populated by Uighurs and other peoples of Turkic descent. (*See* Turkestan, p. 109)

The Golden Horde Region in former Soviet Central Asia, between the Urals and the River Irtysh, that formed the ancient khanate of the Kipchak. It derives its name from the Turkic word *ordas* (Horde) – meaning province, district or specific tribal land. The region was converted to Islam during the reign of Ad Allah Uzbek Khan (*c.* 1313–40) and lent its name to the Turko-Mongol army that swept through Asia into eastern Europe.

Kashgaria *See* East Turkestan

The Maghrib Name given to North Africa by Arab invaders (AD 670–700), which means 'the Land of the Setting Sun' or 'the West' because it marked the western boundaries of the Arab Empire. It is still used by some kilim dealers when referring to items produced in Morocco, Algeria, Tunisia and western Libya (Tripolitania). The original inhabitants of the region were Berbers, but, although large pockets of ethnic Berbers still survive and retain many of their own cultural traditions, the dominant political and cultural influence is Arab. This has been modified to varying degrees by the legacy of Phoenician, Carthaginian, Roman, Vandal, Byzantine, Ottoman Turk, Spanish and French invasions and conquests. (*See* Barbary, p. 108)

Persia Former name for Iran, still widely used in the kilim trade. Older items in particular are often referred to as 'Persian' rather than 'Iranian'. The name was only changed in 1935 and, in this book, 'Persia' and 'Persian' are used when referring to either ethnic Persians or events and kilims produced prior to the 20th century. (*See* Iran, p. 110)

Thrace Traditional name for the western (European) part of Turkey, which was the site of Byzantium and originally extended into the Balkans. (*See* Turkey, p. 113)

Transoxiana *See* Turkestan

Turkestan Literally means 'the Land of the Turks' (Turkic tribesmen or Turkomen) and was applied to the vast, loosely defined area in Central Asia (stretching westwards from the Gobi Desert to the Caspian Sea, traversing the former Soviet Central Asian Republics and northern Afghanistan) where the traditional territories of the mainly nomadic Turkic and Mongol tribesmen lay. Their domination of the region began with the Hun (Mongol tribesmen) invasion, in the 2nd century BC and was firmly established, around AD 400, when a closely related tribal people (the White Huns) established the Ephthalite Empire.

The east and west parts of Turkestan were effectively divided during this period between China, which annexed Kashgaria (East Turkestan) shortly after the fall of the Hun Empire, and the White Huns who ruled Transoxiana (an area in West Turkestan that extends from the Amu Darya or Oxus river to the border of East Turkestan). Both regions fell under the influence of successive invaders over the next 1,500 years and the former inhabitants (Indo-European Tokharians and Yuen-chih nomads of Persian descent) were either displaced or absorbed into the dominant cultures. Transoxiana was conquered, during the 8th century AD, by Arabs (who introduced Islam to the region) and later by the Persian Saminid dynasty, while Kashgaria was under the influence of the Turkic (Uighur) tribesmen for much of this period. However, the rise of the Oghuz or Ghuzz Turkic tribe, during the 10th century, heralded centuries of invasion, conquest, conflict and confusion. It started with the Seljuk Turks' conquest of Transoxiana, Persia, Iraq and much of Asia Minor and was followed over the next few centuries by the conquests of the Mongols under Genghis Khan, the Timuri Turkic tribes under Tamerlane and numerous, ever-changing disputes and rivalries between different Turkic and Mongol factions and tribes. A degree of political and ethnic stability was established in the 19th century when Tashkent was captured by Russia and Transoxiana became the Russian Province of Turkestan. Kashgaria had effectively been under Chinese control since the 18th century, but it was not until the Chinese–Russian treaty, in 1881, that its boundaries were finally established and it became the Sinkiang Province in China. (*See* The former Soviet Caucasian and Central Asian Republics, p. 114, China, p. 120, and East Turkestan, p. 108)

The major contemporary weaving nations

The national boundaries and ethnic mix of most of the major contemporary weaving nations are relatively stable and generally governments and kilim producers recognize the importance of kilim (and pile rug) weaving as a means of maintaining employment and earning foreign currency. Consequently, the appearance, character, quality, cost and availability of kilims from these countries are both relatively predictable and assured. However, the traditionally important producing regions of the former Soviet Caucasian and Central Asian Republics have only recently emerged as independent nations and it may be some years before their kilim production and export arrangements reach previous levels of stability. (*See* The former Soviet Caucasian and Central Asian Republics, p. 114)

Afghanistan (pls 10, 18–20, 26, 29) A land-locked and mountainous country (about the size of Texas), much of it over 4,000 ft (1219 m) above sea level and rising to 25,000 ft (7620 m) in the Hindu Kush Mountains, with large desert regions and intermittent fertile valleys. Its population is around 15 million and is composed of ethnic Afghans (50%), who are politically dominant and Tadjiks (25%) who have a more sedentary, less militaristic lifestyle. There are also a number of Turkic tribesmen, mainly Uzbeks (9%), as well as pockets of Aryans and Mongols, predominantly Hazaras (9%), who live primarily in the Hindu Kush Mountains. Most of the Afghan population are Sunni Muslims. Afghanistan only came into existence as an independent country in 1747, when an Afghan chief, Ahmed Shah, founded a dynasty that remained until a republic was founded in 1973. For much of the previous 1,000 years it had been occupied by one invading force after another, who often used the region as a base for launching their conquests of the richer countries to the east and west.

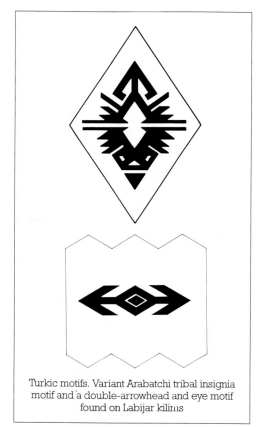

Turkic motifs. Variant Arabatchi tribal insignia motif and a double-arrowhead and eye motif found on Labijar kilims

Afghan kilims are produced by tribal, regional and contemporary workshop groups, and vary considerably in shape, size and appearance. Although kilims are undoubtedly woven by ethnic Afghans (especially contemporary workshop, and to a lesser extent regional, items), there are no purely ethnic Afghan weaving groups and the items that dealers often refer to as traditional Afghan kilims are in fact Turkoman in character, if not actual origin. Tribal weavings are produced by a number of Turkic tribes (mainly Uzbek and Turkoman) and also by Belouch, Aimaq and other closely associated weaving groups. Regional and workshop items fall into two broad categories: Turkoman inspired (sometimes referred to simply as Afghans) and Belouch-Aimaq inspired. Afghanistan has traditionally been a major kilim producer, but the instability of the political situation (both during and since the Afghan-Russian War) continues to affect the regularity of supplies to the West. (*See* Chapter VII: Aimaq, Belouch, Kazakhs, Kutchis, Labijar, Maimana, Mushwani, Qala-i-Nau, Sar-i-Pul, Turkomen and Uzbek)

Bulgaria (pl 14) Balkan country about the size of Ohio with a population of approximately 9 million, comprised primarily of Bulgars (85%) and Turks (8.5%), with a mixture of Slav and other, mainly European, ethnic groups. Most are Orthodox Christians (85%), but there is also a sizeable minority of Muslims (13%). Bulgaria was settled by Slavs in the 6th century and by Turkic Bulgars in the 7th century. Over the next three centuries, the two cultures slowly merged to produce a more unified people who created a powerful empire which survived until the Ottoman Turk invasion in 1396.

Bulgarian kilims are mainly confined to contemporary workshop production aimed at the Western furnishing market. These are generally well made, mainly in the slitweave technique, and feature a wide range of predominantly Turkish and Caucasian designs – often in pastel colours. A small number of more traditional regional items are woven primarily for domestic use, but occasionally find their way on to Western markets. Some Bulgarian workshop kilims are also exported to Turkey where they are sold as Turkish kilims. (*See* Chapter VII: Sarkoy, p. 140)

Iran (pls 15, 16, 21–25, 28, 30, 32, 34, 36, 41) Known as Persia until 1935 and, for many people, the spiritual, if not actual, home of oriental

Current weaving area of Iran, the Caucasus, Central Asia, Afghanistan and Pakistan

rug and kilim weaving. Iran is a vast country, over three times the size of Spain. Its population of about 45 million is composed of a number of ethnic groups, including Persians (63%), Turkic and Belouch tribesmen (19%), Arabs (4%) and Kurds (3%), most of whom live in the more fertile north and north-west of the country. Iran is an Islamic republic that has shown little tolerance in recent years towards Christian, Baha'i and other religious minorities. The vast majority of Iranians (93%) belong to the Shia sect, but there are isolated pockets of Sunnite Muslims, especially among the Kurds and Arabs.

The existence of Persia as an independent country can probably be traced to Cyrus the Great, who united the Medes and the Persians in 549 BC and founded the first Persian Empire. The region was conquered by Alexander the Great in 333 BC and passed on to his general Seleucus (who founded the Seleucid Empire). It regained some of its independence during the next century under the Parthians (north

Persian tribesmen) who were later supplanted, in AD 226, by the Sassanian Persians. The Arab invasion in the 7th century brought Islam to the region, replacing the native Zoroastrian religion, and, although native culture and political autonomy was restored by the 9th century, Islam was by then firmly established in the Persian consciousness. The country was subsequently ruled by a succession of invaders (Seljuk Turks, Mongols and Tamerlane's Turko-Mongol army) from the 11th century to the beginning of the 16th century when the native Safavid dynasty was established by descendants of Sheik Safi-ad-Din. Under the Safavids, Persia achieved unprecedented heights of artistic and cultural expression, and established itself as the epicentre of weaving and textile art. The country fell under Afghan control in 1722, but, in 1857, Britain (which was vying with Russia and France for influence in the region) separated the two countries and Persia was once again ruled – if only in name – by a native (Qajar) dynasty. In 1925, Reza Shah

Pahlavi, a military leader, seized power, changed the country's name to Iran and established the Pahlavi dynasty, which lasted until 1979 when his son and successor, Mohammed Reza Pahlavi, was forced to flee the country, leaving the way for an Islamic republic to be established.

Iranian kilims are woven mainly by tribal and regional groups, but also by some contemporary workshop groups. Iran produces a wider range and diversity of tribal and regional items than almost all the other kilim-weaving countries put together, but the full range of items available in Iran does not always find its way on to Western markets. Similarly, contemporary workshop production is neither as extensive, nor as market focused, as it is, for example, in Turkey or the Balkans. There is also often a grey area between regional and contemporary workshop weaving – some ostensibly regional groups (e.g., Ardebil, Shiraz, Senneh) produce export items, under workshop conditions, that not only retain their regional characteristics but also make few concessions (in design, colour or dimensions) to Western decorative demands. However, if the West's interest in kilims continues to increase, it is likely that a wider range of tribal and regional items will become available, and also that contemporary workshop production will conform more to Western furnishing requirements. (*See* Chapter VII: Afshar, Ardebil, Azerbaijan, Bakhtiari, Belouch, Bidjar, Garmsar, Hamadan, Harsin, Kerman, Khamseh, Kurds, Lurs, Qashga'i, Senneh, Shahsavan, Shiraz, Talish, Veramin and Zarand)

Morocco (pls 7, 13, 17) A constitutional monarchy, slightly larger than California, and is the most westerly country of the Maghrib. Its population of about 24 million is mainly Arab (65%), but also contains the highest percentage of Berbers (30%) in North Africa. Berbers were the original inhabitants, but, after relatively short-lived occupations by Romans and Carthaginians, they were gradually supplanted as the major ethnic group by Arabs, who invaded in the 7th century and have occupied the country ever since, although a Berber Empire (the Moors) ruled most of north-west Africa and Spain from Morocco during the 11th and 12th centuries. During the 19th and early 20th centuries, Spain and France ruled different parts of the country and it was not until

1956 that Morocco once again became an independent country.

Moroccan kilims are produced by tribal, regional and contemporary workshop weaving groups. Morocco is the largest exporter of kilims from North Africa and, unlike their pile rugs (which are often garish and poorly constructed), Moroccan kilims are generally both attractive and of good quality. (*See* Chapter VII: Arab weaving groups, Azrou, Berber, Boujaad, Hanbel, Oudzem, Taznakht, Tiffelt)

Romania (pl 8) Largest of the Balkan countries, slightly smaller than Italy, with a population of approximately 23 million, composed of ethnic Romanians (80%), Hungarians (8%) and Germans (1.6%). They are mainly Orthodox Christians (80%), but also Catholics (6%). During the 1st millennium BC, Proto-Thracian invaders merged with the native inhabitants (about whom almost nothing is known) and a few centuries later the region was occupied by Slavs and Dacian tribes from the Danube Valley. It became part of the Roman Empire, from AD 106 to 271, and as part of a general Romanization the Romanian language (based on Latin with numerous Slav words) began to evolve. In common with the other Balkan countries, Romania was dominated by the Ottoman Empire from the 15th century and it was not until 1878 that it freed itself from Turkish control and became an independent kingdom. Despite centuries of Turkish rule, Romania managed to retain its ethnic, cultural and religious integrity to a much higher degree than its Balkan neighbours.

Romanian kilims combine their own folk-weaving traditions with the legacy of Turkish rug and kilim production. The vast majority of Romanian kilims are contemporary workshop items made specifically for export, but some more traditional regional items are also produced – usually for the domestic and tourist markets. They mainly use slit-weave technique and employ a range of Turkish, Caucasian and sometimes Iranian designs, often in slightly more pastel colour schemes, as well as traditional folk-art and other Romanian or Turkish-Romanian designs. Romania has been the most important weaving country in the Balkans for most of this century. However, the full horror of Romania's recent history only began to emerge after the overthrow of the Ceausescu regime, in 1989, and it may be some years before kilim

Above: current weaving areas of Turkey and the Balkans. *Left*: North Africa

production, export and classification are stabilized. (*See* Chapter VII)

Tunisia A republic, about the size of Missouri, situated on the eastern coast of the Maghrib. Its population (of around 7 million) is a well-integrated mixture of Arab and Berber (98%), although there are some Jews, Turks and Europeans, the vast majority of whom are Muslim. Tunisia is the site of ancient Carthage (founded by the Phoenicians in 814 BC), which became the most important port in North Africa and subsequently the centre of Carthaginian civilization, until it was destroyed by the Romans, in 146 BC. The entire region became part of the Arab Empire (in the 7th century), resulting in widespread Arab settlement and the introduction of Islam. Tunisia was absorbed into the Ottoman Empire, in 1574, and became a French protectorate, in 1881, before gaining its independence in 1956.

Tunisian kilims are similar to Moroccan items, but, although tribal in character, they are generally produced and marketed according to regional styles, rather than specific tribal affinities. They are nevertheless generally attractive, well made and authentically tribal in appearance. (*See* Chapter VII: El Jem, Gafsa, Matmata, Oudref, Redeyef and Sidi Bou Zid)

Turkey (pls 4, 5, 9, 11, 31, 35, 37) A republic, approximately twice the size of California, that straddles both Europe and Asia. European Turkey (Thrace) covers an area slightly smaller than Belgium and is divided by the Bosporus and the Sea of Marmara from the vastly larger Asian part of the country (Anatolia), which was the home of some of the world's first agricultural societies (Phrygians, Hittites and Lydians) who flourished from the 3rd to the 1st millennium BC. The region's earliest external cultural influences came from ancient Greece and the Roman Empire. The Arab invasion in the 7th century brought Islam to the country and successive Turkoman and Mongol conquests (from the 11th century to the beginnings of the Ottoman Empire in the 13th century) laid the ethnic and the cultural foundation of modern Turkey. The current population of around

50 million is composed of ethnic Turks (85%), who are themselves a mixture of Mediterranean, Turkoman and Mongol stock, and Kurds (12%). Turkey was synonymous with the Ottoman Empire until its formation into a republic in 1923 under the guidance of Kemal Ataturk (Mustapha Kemal), who is considered to be the founder of modern Turkey.

Turkish kilims are produced almost exclusively by regional and contemporary workshop groups (many of whom specialize in items of tribal appearance). The Yoruks are the only generally recognized nomadic weaving group, although there are a number of mainly Kurdish nomadic and semi-nomadic weaving tribes in the east of the country. Turkey is the largest and most consistent supplier of kilims to the West – primarily because the Turkish authorities and kilim producers have managed (since the late 1970s) to restructure their weaving industry so that it successfully combines modern production and marketing techniques with traditional weaving standards. This results in items that are authentic in character and appearance and also compatible with Western decorative tastes. In essence, Turkish kilim production can be broadly divided into regional groups, usually village or provincial town based, who weave items that conform to a traditional tribal or localized style (e.g., Karapinar, Van, Malatya); and contemporary workshop groups, normally situated in the larger cities and urban centres (e.g., Bergama, Usak, Izmir), who produce a wide range of authentic-looking items based on the kilims from a number of traditional weaving groups including Turkish, Caucasian and, occasionally, Iranian. (*See* Chapter VII: Adana, Afyon, Aksaray, Antalya, Aydin, Balikesir, Bergama, Corum, Denizli, Erzurum, Esme, Fethiye, Gaziantep, Karapinar, Kars, Kayseria, Keles, Konya, Malatya, Manastir, Mut, Nigde, Obruk, Reyhanli, Sarkoy, Sivas, Sivrihisar, Ushak, Van and Yuruks)

The former Soviet Caucasian and Central Asian Republics

The dissolution of the Soviet Union has resulted in dramatic changes to the political, social and cultural stability of its former Caucasian and Central Asian Republics. Border disputes and ethnic conflicts have arisen in several regions, which have disrupted the existing production and export channels, and made it extremely difficult to predict either the future availability of kilims from these regions or their character and weaving categories. Some of these fledgling nations seem to be experiencing a relatively smooth transition to independence, whereas others appear to be destined to several years of social and political unrest. However, the history of kilim weaving has unfolded against an almost unrelenting backdrop of conflict and instability and yet, with few exceptions, the weavers have invariably adapted to the existing circumstances and continued to produce items that are often either unchanged or have successfully incorporated elements of their new situation. Consequently, allowing for a period of readjustment, it is probable that kilim weaving will continue to play an important role in the social and economic life of Caucasian and Central Asian weaving groups.

In the interim, exports from these countries are likely to be somewhat erratic, both in the numbers produced and the countries to which they are exported. For example, at any given time, Armenian rugs may be widely available in the United States, but hard to find in France. Similarly, British dealers may still be able to obtain regular supplies from their personal contacts in Uzbekistan, but find greater difficulty in exporting items through official channels in Kirghizstan, while, during the same period, German or Swedish dealers may find that the reverse is true. Future diplomatic relationships between individual importing and exporting nations may also affect the availability of certain items.

Soviet decentralization Two main classifications of local autonomy, frequently along ethnic divisions, were used throughout the Soviet Union and are denoted by the suffixes (SSR and ASSR) after the regional name – for example, Armenia SSR and Tartar ASSR.

SSR (Soviet Socialist Republics) are constitutional republics, with their own elected government, national representatives and legal and fiscal powers.

ASSR (Autonomous Soviet Socialist Regions) are semi-governing regions within an existing SSR. For instance, Nagorny Karabagh ASSR is a quasi-autonomous region within the larger Azerbaijan SSR.

CIS (Commonwealth of Independent States) is the name adopted, in 1991, for the loose federation of former Soviet Republics that replaced the old Soviet Union.

The former Soviet Caucasian Republics

The republics were formed according to the ethnic group in the majority (e.g., Armenians in Armenia, Azerbaijanis in Azerbaijan), but no attempt was made to relocate isolated ethnic groups (i.e., a minority of Armenians in Azerbaijan) and vice versa. Since independence, however, there has been a series of often violent conflicts between these respective ethnic groups; the majority wanting to expel the alien minority from their new country and the minority seeking to merge their traditional territory into their kinsman's adjacent republic. The situation is further complicated by pockets of Kurds, Russians, Ossetians and other ethnic and religious minorities, who now find themselves living in increasingly nationalistic states and it may be several years, even decades, before the underlying conflicts are finally resolved. Interim kilim production and export has understandably been adversely affected by the ongoing climate of conflict and uncertainty.

Caucasian kilims Can be divided into three main periods of production: traditional Caucasian kilims, Soviet Caucasian kilims and independent Caucasian Republic kilims.

Traditional Caucasian kilims

The kilims and pile rugs woven in the Caucasus, during the 18th, 19th and early 20th centuries, before its assimilation into the Soviet Union, are generally considered to be among the finest examples of regional/tribal weaving ever produced and are of great importance to collectors, dealers and contemporary kilim producers. Several items dating from the 19th and early 20th centuries are still on the market and traditional Caucasian designs continue to be used by a number of contemporary (mainly workshop) weaving groups.

During the 16th and 17th centuries, the Caucasus was divided into dozens of independent khanates – ranging in size from a few small villages to areas larger than London or New York. Each was presided over by a local khan, many of whom were tied politically and culturally to the Persian Empire (which elevated carpet weaving to unprecedented heights

Amulet/medallion taken from a traditional Caucasian Daghestan kilim

of artistic and structural achievement) and many of the Caucasian khans established their own carpet workshops in an attempt to emulate the sophistication of the Persian court. Weavers with small, delicate fingers were needed to produce these extremely intricate court carpets (*see* p. 10) and so girls, often as young as seven, were drafted from their villages into the khan's workshops. Once they reached maturity (and their hands grew too big for exceptionally fine weaving) they returned to their villages, married and began weaving simplified versions of court carpet designs from memory. Over the next 200 years, these bolder, more abstract renditions of sophisticated, Persian-inspired designs merged with the various local weaving traditions to form the basis of the folk weaving that is often referred to as the golden age of Traditional Caucasian weaving.

Traditional Caucasian weaving groups (pls 1, 39, 40) Kilims were produced during the 18th, 19th and early 20th centuries in hundreds of villages throughout the entire Caucasus region. Each village or collection of villages is associated with items that conformed to an overall style and a repertoire of designs. For example, kilims classified as Kazakhs have a character and appearance associated with items produced in the village of the same name. However, there is sometimes little or no evidence to support these attributions and they need to be treated as traditional classifications, rather than exact references to where an item was actually made. The main traditional weaving groups are located in:

Baku, a town in Azerbaijan, on the Caspian Sea, believed to have been a major centre for *zilli* kilims and also items that employ repeating *botehs* and other tiny geometric or stylized floral motifs.

Borchaly, a region in Georgia, usually considered to be part of the Kazakh weaving group, although Borchaly kilims are generally less heraldic – featuring smaller repeating medallions and geometric forms.

Daghestan, a region north of Azerbaijan, associated particularly with intricate, all-over designs based on repeating geometric or floral motifs.

Derbend, a city and district on the Caspian Sea, is a sub-group of Daghestans, which is associated with the production of medium quality items in a variety of general Caucasian styles.

Erivan or Yerevan, a major city in Armenia that acted as a marketing and distribution centre for Armenian items and subsequently lent its name to otherwise unattributed kilims woven in the region.

Gianja, a village in Azerbaijan associated with kilims that are very similar to Kazakhs, but employ more complex compositions, often featuring all-over star motifs.

Karabagh, a region in south-west Azerbaijan (but with a majority of ethnic Armenians) usually associated with European-style floral designs. Karabaghs were produced in a wide range of other designs (including *zilli*, Adler and Cloudband Kazakhs) and woven in various techniques (e.g., slitweave, *jajim*, *verneh*). They are now made in Turkey and Bulgaria.

Kazakh, a village in western Azerbaijan noted for producing kilims with large, overtly heraldic central medallions – often known as Eagle (Adler) Kazakhs or Cloudband Kazakhs, etc., depending on the specific medallion – although many items classified as Kazakhs were in fact made across the border in Armenia and Georgia. Slitweave was the most common technique, but *zilli* and *verneh* were also made.

Kuba (pl 39), a town in north-east Azerbaijan associated particularly with pole-medallion and repeating geometric designs, woven mainly in slitweave and *soumak* techniques.

Shirvan (pl 40), a district in central Azerbaijan associated especially with diamond medallions and banded, repeating geometric designs, woven predominantly in slitweave and occasionally weft wrapping.

Talish, Mogan and Lenkoran weaving groups are associated with an area of southern Azerbaijan. They are noted for producing items with intricate, repeating designs (often with 'S' motifs) in a number of flatweaving techniques, including *jajim* and *soumak*.

Soviet Caucasian kilims (pls 3, 12)

During the Soviet period traditional regional kilims were still woven for the domestic market, but most of the items exported to the West were of contemporary workshop origin.

Soviet Caucasian workshop kilims (pl 12) Generally of good quality, attractive and produced in a range of traditional designs, but they normally lack the subtle artistry of composition, colour and articulation that typified traditional Caucasian kilims. Soviet workshop kilims were produced in different parts of the Caucasus and usually marketed under the names of the traditional weaving groups (Kazakh, Shirvan, etc.) whose designs were used rather than where they were made. They normally fall into the low-to-medium price bracket, are still fairly widely available and make excellent furnishing items.

Soviet Caucasian regional kilims (pl 3) Kilims – especially those from Armenia and Azerbaijan – that are closer in appearance and character to traditional Caucasian items. They are comparatively scarce and fall into the medium-to-high bracket. (*See* Independent Caucasian Republic kilims)

Independent Caucasian Republic kilims

The new market freedom throughout the republics, coupled with the lessening of production controls, may possibly result in a more diverse and unpredictable kilim weaving industry. There may be a return to more traditional regional weaving, but almost certainly in the short term the respective prices, availability, character and classifications of the kilims from each republic will remain inconsistent.

Armenia (Republic of) (pl 3 and similar to pl 1) A mountainous, sub-tropical region in the south-east corner of the Caucasus, approximately the size of Belgium, that lies at the heart of what was once ancient Armenia. Its current population (of around 4 million) is comprised of Christian Armenians (90%), Muslim Azerbaijanis (5%), Kurds (2%) and Russians (2%). The region was occupied by the Red Army in 1920 (only eight years after gaining its independence from Turkey) and incorporated into the Soviet Union, as a constitutional republic (SSR), in 1936. Demands for a union with Nagorny Karabagh (an autonomous region in neighbouring Azerbaijan with a majority of Armenians) led to open conflict between the two states' ethnic and religious groups (1989–90), which resulted in Armenia declaring its independence, in 1991, as part of the CIS.

Armenian regional kilims are based on the traditional Caucasian items woven in the area, including the ethnic Armenian district of Nagorny Karabagh in Azerbaijan. Known locally as *karpets*, they are generally extremely well made, using a variety of slitweave, *soumak* and supplementary weft techniques, in a wide range of mainly medallion and to a lesser extent folk-art, floral and all-over designs. They are similar to Azerbaijani kilims – but perhaps even more heraldic and strongly coloured – with elements of Christian symbolism and Armenian folk-art motifs incorporated into the design. *Zilli*, Vishapogorg (dragon) and Karabagh items are closely associated with Armenia and a number of bags, animal trappings and artefacts was also made. Most Armenian regional weaving falls into the medium-to-high price bracket. (*See* Traditional Caucasian weaving groups: Erivan, Karabagh and Kazakh, p. 116)

Azerbaijan (Republic of) (pls 39, 40 and similar to pls 1–3) A mountainous and semi-desert region of the south-east Caucasus, approximately the size of Scotland, that incorporates the Nagorny Karabagh ASSR and has a population of around 7 million which is composed of Sunnite Islamic Azerbaijanis (78%), Christian Armenians (8%, mainly in Nagorny-Karabagh) and Russians (8%). Azerbaijan was occupied by the Red Army in 1920 and incorporated into the Soviet Union, as a constitutional republic (SSR), in 1936. The growth of nationalism, during the late 1980s, was spearheaded by the Azerbaijan Popular Front and erupted into civil war between ethnic Azerbaijanis and Armenians. The conflict spread to open confrontation with the Armenian SSR and led to the insertion of peace-keeping Russian troops and Azerbaijan's decision, in 1991, to declare its independence and join the CIS.

Azerbaijani regional kilims evolved from the traditional Caucasian items woven in the area, especially Shirvan, Kuba, Gianja and Kazakh. They are produced using a variety of weaving techniques – e.g., slitweave, plainweave (*palas*), *soumak, verneh, zilli* and *jajim* – and employ an extensive range of traditional, mainly geometric, designs. Azerbaijani kilims are similar to those made in Armenia, but tend towards a darker palette and, with the exception of Karabaghs, are usually more overtly Islamic in design. They also share a close compositional affinity with the items made by ethnic Azerbaijanis in the bordering Iranian Province of Azerbaijan. A large number of bags, animal trappings and artefacts are also woven. Azerbaijan is the largest and most varied producer of kilims in the Caucasus and most traditional items fall into the medium-to-high price bracket. (*See* Traditional Caucasian weaving groups: Baku, Borchaly, Gianja, Karabagh, Kazakh, Kuba and Shirvan, p. 116)

Daghestan (ASSR) Region of mountains and valleys, slightly smaller than Denmark. With a population of approximately 2 million it is arguably the most cosmopolitan area of the Caucasus, with over 30 identifiable national and ethnic groups – drawn from other parts of the Caucasus, Central Asia and the Middle East – who speak numerous languages and dialects, and have a diversity of religious allegiances. Daghestan was annexed by Russia from Iran, in 1723, and, after the Russian revolution, was established as an ASSR, in 1923, within the Russian Federation.

Daghestan regional kilims are known locally as *davaghins*. They often have a deep blue field decorated with complex medallion forms (*rukzals*) – or other repeating geometric motifs – in deep or brownish red. A number of weaving techniques are employed – mainly *soumak*, slitweave and plainweave (*palas*) – and, in addition to kilims, a wide variety of bags, animal trappings, artefacts and cotton flatweaves are also made. Daghestan kilims are generally less brightly coloured than Armenian and Azerbaijani items, but employ warmer reds and blues than their neighbours in Georgia. The city of Derbend, on the Caspian Sea, opened a school of carpet making, in 1931, which became a forerunner of Soviet work-shop production in the region. Daghestan kilims are not generally considered to be of the same aesthetic or structural quality as those produced in Armenia and Azerbaijan, but are still highly collectable and normally fall into the medium-to-high price bracket. (*See* Traditional Caucasian weaving groups: Daghestan and Derbend, p. 116)

Georgia (Republic of) Fertile, mainly agricultural region, about the size of Ireland, in the north-west of the Caucasus, that also incorporates the South Ossetian ASSR (part of Ossetia, the traditional homeland of an Ossetian-speaking minority) and the Abkhazian ASSR (home to the Abkhazians, a minority group of uncertain ethnic origins). The total population of the region (around 5 million) is composed of ethnic Georgians (69%), Armenians (9%), Russians (7%), Azerbaijanis (5%), Ossetians (2%) and Abkhazians (2%). Orthodox Christianity is the dominant religion among ethnic Georgians, Russians and Armenians, but the Abkhazians were converted to Islam during the 17th century and there are a few other, mainly Islamic, minorities. Georgia was an independent republic before its invasion by Soviet troops, in 1921, and its incorporation into the Soviet Trans-Caucasian Republic (1922–36). It was given SSR status in 1936 and, after a period of ethnic conflict (mainly as a result of Ossetian and Abkhazian attempts at secession), Georgia declared its independence in 1991 and became part of the CIS.

Georgian regional kilims are known locally as *pardaghis* and are generally less colourful and more primitive in appearance than other Caucasian kilims. The Georgian palette is dominated by dark blues, black, deep reddish orange and browns, contrasted with lighter blues, pink, yellow ochre and white. Designs vary from naturalistic (usually floral, similar to Karabaghs), through a wide range of typically Caucasian and Iranian designs, to very simple – almost folk-art – renditions of stylized animal, bird, floral and symbolic forms (usually crosses, diamonds and stars). Georgia is one of the main producers of kilims in the Caucasus, but most are made either for personal use or for sale on the domestic market and very few have been exported to the West – comparatively

few bags and artefacts are produced. Most Georgian items fall into the medium-to-high bracket.

The former Soviet Central Asian Republics
(pls 18, 20, 42)

The inhabitants of the former Soviet Central Asian Republics are mainly descendants of the Turkic and Mongol tribesmen who settled in the region, following a succession of invasions and migrations, from the 11th century onwards. Their traditional territory was known as Turkestan and, during the 18th and 19th centuries, was effectively split between Russia and China. After the Russian Revolution, the new Soviet Union devised a policy of dividing Russian (or West) Turkestan into separate states, which reflected their respective concentrations of individual ethnic and cultural groups. This was implemented at different times between 1920 and 1945. (*See* Turkestan, p. 109, and Turks, Turkomen and Turkic tribes, p. 49)

Kilim production in Central Asia was not disrupted, either by the advent of, or the dissolution of, the Soviet Union, to the extent that it was in the Caucasus. Contemporary workshop production was established by the Soviet authorities in different parts of the region, but they were mainly confined to making pile rugs and, although some workshop kilims were made, most of the items sold in the West were of regional or tribal origin.

Future production is extremely difficult to predict, but, despite some ongoing ethnic and regional conflict, it is probable that Central Asian weaving will change very little over the next few decades. However, the respective supplies and prices of items from each republic are likely to be erratic until new export channels have been established.

Soviet Central Asian kilims are generally almost identical in character and appearance to the traditional items produced by each ethnic or regional group. (*See* Chapter VII: Karakalpaks, Kazakhs, Kirghiz, Tadjiks, Tartars, Turkomen and Uzbeks)

Karakalpak (ASSR) A quasi-autonomous region, slightly larger than Georgia (USA), situated south of the Aral Sea, that was the traditional home of the Karakalpaks. The region was conquered by Russia, in 1867, and, in 1926, made an autonomous region within Kazakhstan. Subsequently, it was transferred to the Soviet republic in 1930, made into a republic, in 1932, and finally attached to Uzbekistan in 1936. Its current population of 1 million is mainly Karakalpak, with Uzbek, Russian and other, mainly Turkic, ethnic minorities. (*See* Chapter VII: Karakalpaks and Tartars)

Kazakhstan (Republic of) A vast region, nearly four times the size of Texas, stretching from the Caspian Sea in the west to China and Mongolia in the east that is the traditional homeland of the Kazakh nomads. The region was ruled by the Mongols during the 13th century and later became a collection of independent khanates or tribal territories. They were dominated by the largely nomadic tribesmen who had entered the region as part of a succession of Turkic and Mongol invasions and migrations. Russia conquered the territory in the 18th century and, in 1922, established Kazakhstan as an autonomous region. It was made into a full republic, in 1936, but Kruschev's desire to utilize virgin agricultural land, during the 1950s and 1960s, initiated a vast influx of ethnic Russians and Ukrainians. This resulted in ethnic Kazakhs becoming a racial minority in their own land, whose current population of 16 million is comprised of Russians (41%), Kazakhs (36%), Ukrainians (6%) and other, mainly Turkic, minorities. After violent nationalist rallies in the late 1980s, Kazakhstan seceded from the Soviet Union in 1991 and became an independent republic with the CIS. (*See* Chapter VII: Kazakhs)

Note Kazakh is also a town in former Soviet Azerbaijan which lends its name to one of the traditional Caucasian weaving groups. (*See* Traditional Caucasian kilims, p. 115)

Kirghizstan (Republic of) A mountainous and steppe region, about the size of South Dakota, that was traditionally known as 'Kirghizia' (the territory of the Kirghiz nomads). The region was conquered by Russia in 1864 and made part of the Turkestan Republic (1917–24) before becoming an independent constitutional Soviet republic in 1936. The population of approximately 4 million is made up of ethnic Kirghiz (52%), Russians (21%) and other, mainly Turkic, groups, who, with the exception of the Christian Russians, are predominantly Sunnite Muslims. Kirghizstan became an independent republic with the CIS in 1991. (*See* Chapter VII: Kirghiz)

Tadzhikistan or Tajikistan (Republic of) Smallest of the former Soviet Central Asian Republics, about the size of England and Wales, that was formed, in 1924, from the ethnic Tajik population, in what was formerly the Bokhara region of Turkestan, and became a constitutional republic in 1929. The current population of approximately 5 million is composed mainly of ethnic Tajiks (59%), Uzbeks (23%) and Russians and Ukrainians (11%). It seceded from the Soviet Union, in 1991, and joined the CIS. (*See* Chapter VII: Tadjiks)

Tartar or Tatar (ASSR) Autonomous region in the Middle and Upper Volga Valley, slightly smaller than Scotland, that was part of the Bulgar (Volga-Kama) state during the 10th and 13th centuries. The area was first conquered by the Mongols and then by the Russians in 1552. Tartars have lived in the region for centuries, but it only became their official homeland after the Tartar ASSR was formed in 1920. In 1944, ethnic Tartars were deported from their other territories in the Crimea both to the Tartar ASSR and to Uzbekistan. It now has a population of around 3½ million composed mainly of Tartars, but also of Russian, Uzbek and other minority groups. (*See* Chapter VII: Tartars)

Turkmenistan (Republic of) A mainly desert area, slightly larger than Norway, that was one of the most westerly territories of the Turkic tribes and, in 1925, was formed into a constitutional republic (SSR). The population of around 3½ million is composed mainly of Turkomen (69%) or Turkmenians as they are now officially known, Russians (9%), Uzbeks (3%) and Kazakhs (3%), with the exception of the Russians, they are almost exclusively Sunnite Muslims. Turkmenistan seceded from the Soviet Union in 1991 and joined the CIS. (*See* Chapter VII: Turkomen)

Uzbekistan (Republic of) (pl 42) An area of deserts, oases, valleys and mountains, approximately the size of Sweden. The region was conquered by Russia, between 1865 and 1876, and formed into an independent republic in 1925. Although Uzbekistan was conceived as an official homeland for the Uzbeks, it also contains the Karakalpak ASSR and, in 1944, Stalin enforced the relocation of Mesketian Turks (from Georgia) and Tartars (from the Crimea). It is the most densely populated of the former Soviet republics, with around 19 million people, composed of Uzbeks (69%), Russians (11%), Tajiks (4%), Tartars (4%), Mesketian Turks and other minority groups – most of

Various Turkoman *gul* design motifs. *From left*: cruxiform secondary *gul*; Tekke *gul*; variant Yomut diamond *gul*

whom, with the exception of the Russians, are Sunnite Muslims. Uzbekistan seceded from the Soviet Union in 1991 and joined the CIS. (*See* Chapter VII: Tartars and Uzbeks)

The minor weaving nations

Albania Smallest of the Balkan countries, only slightly larger than Sicily, and has a population of just over 3 million people of Mediterranean, Slav, Turkoman and mixed European descent. The country has been traditionally Muslim since the 15th century when it was occupied by the Ottoman Turks, but in 1967 religious worship was banned by the hardline Communist regime.

Albanian kilims are mainly produced in government-sponsored workshops, but do not appear with great regularity on Western markets. In price, quality and appearance they are similar to Bulgarian items.

Algeria Largest country of The Maghrib (North Africa), over three times the size of Texas. Most of its population of 25 million people (75% Arab and 25% Berber) live in the north, between the coast and the Saharan Mountains – the vast central and southern part of the country, including much of the Sahara Desert, is relatively sparsely populated.

Algerian kilims are woven by Berbers and Arabs and are similar to those produced in Morocco and Tunisia, but comparatively few reach Western markets.

China The third largest country in the world, covering most of the landmass of South-East Asia, that now incorporates the former independent territories of Manchuria, southern (Inner) Mongolia, Tibet and East Turkestan. It has a population of over 1 billion people, the vast majority of whom are ethnic Han Chinese (94%), but there are also significant minorities of Manchus, Mongols and Tibetans, as well as Uighurs and other Turkic tribes. Most of the annexed territories (even Tibet which was only occupied in the 1950s) have been heavily settled by the Han Chinese and the Chinese government has pursued an often ruthless policy of Sinofication. However, Sinkiang Province (formerly East Turkestan) has remained relatively unaffected – probably because its geographical remoteness and climatic severity proved to be both unsuitable for the mainly agrarian Chinese settlers and extremely difficult to police. It is still populated largely by Uighur and other Turkic and Mongolian tribesmen, many of whom continue to practise a nomadic and semi-nomadic way of life.

Chinese workshop kilims are produced specifically for Western markets and frequently employ European floral designs (often based on the old Bessarabian kilims). They are well made, usually small to medium in size, and fall into the medium price bracket.

Chinese tribal and regional kilims are made in Sinkiang Province by Uighur and other, mainly Turkic, tribal groups. They are similar to Turkoman weavings, but have a softer (more Chinese palette) and often incorporate elements of Buddhist and Taoist symbolism. They rarely appear on Western markets and usually fall into the low-to-medium price bracket. They are often marketed as Kashgaria kilims.

Greece Occupies the southern end of the Balkan peninsula and was part of the Byzantine Empire until the 15th century when it was occupied by the Ottoman Turks – only freeing itself from Turkish dominance after the War of Independence (1821–29). It has little connection with the kilim-producing world either ethnically or religiously (with 98.5% of the population being Greek and 97% being Orthodox Christian), but years of Turkish rule have left a flatweaving legacy that manifests itself not only in traditional Greek flatweaves, but also in copies of old Turkish kilims that are often sold to unsuspecting tourists as genuine antiques left over from the Turkish occupation.

Iraq Comprises most of Mesopotamia and part of the Maghrib and is the site of the ancient Babylonian and Assyrian civilizations. It is slightly larger than California and has a population of around 15 million which is mainly Arab (75%), but is also made up of other ethnic groups, including Kurds (15%) and Turkomen (5%). Islam was brought to Iraq in the 7th century and it became part of the Ottoman Empire in 1638. Unlike most countries in the region, Iraq was fairly evenly divided between Shia (55%) and Sunnite (40%) Muslims, but, in 1975, the predominantly Sunnite Muslim Kurds were defeated in their efforts to secure a homeland and have since been subjected to appalling persecution at the instigation of Saddam Hussein and the ruling Baath Arab Socialist Party. Similar campaigns have been waged against the Marsh Arabs and other ethnic, political and religious minorities.

Iraqi kilims are produced mainly for the domestic market or for personal use and very few are sold in the West. The main exceptions are Kurdish and Marsh Arab weavings, which are sometimes available in the West, although a number of Iraqi Kurdish items are marketed under the general heading of Kurd or Kurdistan kilims, as they are often smuggled across the border and sold in Iran. Marsh Arab flatweaves are intricate and brightly coloured and are usually either *namads* (felt rugs) or are woven in variations of *jajim* and tapestry techniques.

Pakistan (pls 19, 26, 33) Acquired dominion status, in 1947 – when the British withdrew from India – as one of two areas dominated by Islam (West and East Pakistan) that would be unified into the self-governing state of Pakistan, despite being separated by a thousand miles of India. Pakistan became a republic in 1956, but growing conflict between the powerful West and the desperately poor East resulted, in 1971, in a war of secession, in which India intervened – the outcome was the formation of two totally independent states. East Pakistan became Bangladesh and West Pakistan retained the name Pakistan and is now an Islamic republic, slightly larger than Texas. Pakistan shares a 5,000-year history with the rest of the Indian sub-continent and, although it has its own long-established pile rug weaving heritage, its importance in kilim production only began to emerge during the Afghan-Russian War (1979–89) when in excess of 2 million refugees flooded across the border, bringing with them their kilim weaving traditions. Pakistan is now an increasingly important kilim-producing country – not only because weaving provides a valuable source of revenue for the Afghan, Belouch and other tribal refugees, but also because Pakistan is one of the few stable countries in the region, making it relatively easy for Western dealers to import Pakistani goods. In addition to items that are now being made within its borders, Pakistan also acts as a marketing centre for goods from Afghanistan, Uzbekistan and other central Asian countries. It is impossible to predict exactly how kilim production will evolve in Pakistan in the early 21st century, but Pakistani producers and dealers have shown themselves to be very adept at providing pile rugs for the Western market and, if the West's interest in kilims continues to expand, it is probable that Pakistan will increasingly become a centre of kilim production.

Pakistani kilims are almost entirely confined to items produced by the Belouch and related tribesmen in Baluchistan Province and those made by a range of refugees from Afghanistan since the Afghan-Russian War. These refugees have settled mainly around the north-west frontier town of Peshawar and further south near Quelta. They are predominantly Belouch, Aimaq, Afghan and Turkoman and produce items that correspond to traditional structures and designs. (*See* Chapter VII: Aimaq, Belouch, Turkomen and Uzbek)

Hook or *cengel* border arrangement

Weaving groups

This chapter contains information on all the major kilim-weaving groups, listed under their most generally applied names. However, it is important to recognize that the naming of kilims is sometimes arbitrary and some dealers may use alternative names. This may be either because they do not know an item's true origins and consequently employ a generic (e.g., Hanbel) or a vague tribal name (e.g., Kurdish) or because they want to make a kilim appear more unusual and exotic and so they use the name of an obscure sub-tribe (e.g., Maldari).

Tribal and trans-national weaving groups

This section includes all the major tribal kilim weavers. The tribal groups not included either produce very few, if any, kilims (e.g., Yalameh) or their items are almost always marketed under the name of a general weaving group. For example, a number of small tribal groups in the Khorassan Province of eastern Iran produce items that are difficult to attribute specifically and so are often classified as simply belonging to the general Khorassan weaving group.

Trans-national weaving groups are homogeneous ethnic groups (e.g., the Kurds), who inhabit several regions and may be involved in the production of tribal, regional and occasionally workshop kilims, depending on the location. Their kilims are nevertheless sufficiently similar to each other to be considered to have an overall Kurdish allegiance.

Afshar or Awshar (pls 22, 23) Nomadic and semi-nomadic tribesmen of Oghuz Turkoman descent who inhabit four widely separated regions in Iran. In the 15th century, the Afshar was one of the seven tribes who composed the Kyzylbash (red-head) federation – a military-political grouping, of mainly Dervish influence, so named after their red turbans – responsible for promoting the first Safavid Shah, Ismail, to the Persian throne. However, in the 16th century, the Afshar leader attempted to murder Shah Abbas's mother and so sections of the tribe were forcibly dispersed to some of the more inhospitable regions of the country. The Afshar are one of the most important tribal weaving groups in Iran, producing a wide and diverse range of attractive, well-made and highly collectable items, as well as influencing regional weaving (especially in Kerman). They are more closely associated with pile rugs than kilims, but are still a significant source of Iranian tribal kilims.

Afshar kilims have a number of unifying features – they are usually boldly geometric in design, with a dominant palette of deep reds, blues, orange and yellow ochres, employ cotton warps and have a fairly heavy-duty construction. Afshar kilims, bags, animal trappings and other artefacts are reasonably widely available on Western markets and retail predominantly within the low-to-medium price bracket. However, each localized Afshar group has absorbed some of the weaving traditions of the host region and there are now some clear distinctions between the Afshar kilims produced in different parts of Iran.

Azerbaijan Afshars are produced by mainly settled tribesmen. They are very similar to other north-west Iranian weavings: normally fairly large and rectangular (although some smaller items are made), decorated with bold, repeating medallions on open grounds and employ the usual Afshar palette with hints of white. They are usually woven in slitweave and occasionally double interlock.

Kerman Afshars (pl 22) are produced by the largest, most important and accomplished of all the Afshar splinter groups who were banished to this mountainous region of southern Iran in the 16th and 17th centuries. Many ethnic Afshars have settled and intermarried into the local community – strongly influencing Kerman regional weaving – but a substantial number have retained their nomadic lifestyle and continue to make authentic tribal kilims, bags, animal trappings and other artefacts. The designs include a wide range of medallion, all-over geometric and banded designs, often with animals, people, tribal talismen, small rosettes or floral heads (sometimes in white cotton) and a variety of geometric forms as infill motifs. They are predominantly rectangular, ranging in size from small to large – employ the standard Afshar palette, often with additions of white and occasionally green – and are woven in slitweave, double interlock, weft wrapping and dovetailing. Items produced in the areas around the towns of Sirjan, Jiruft and Baft are sometimes classified as sub-groups of Kerman Afshars and marketed under these names. Sirjans are very similar to the majority of Kermans, but tend to be especially finely woven and to contain more than the average amount of white cotton to highlight elements in the design. Jirufts and Bafts are very similar to each other and are only distinguished from the majority of Kermans by their preferred use of crenellated medallions and extended spandrels or field-surround (Jirufts) and banded designs (Bafts).

Khorassan Afshars are made by semi-nomadic and settled descendants of the tribes banished to the north-east corner of Iran in the 16th and 17th centuries. Some of their kilims (especially those produced by settled weavers) have merged into a general Khorassan style, but distinctive tribal kilims, bags, animal trappings and other artefacts are still made. These are usually small and rectangular, employ the typical Afshar palette, but differ from other Afshar kilims in that they often feature small geometric motifs – perhaps crenellated or zig-zag – as part of a medallion or banded design. Slitweaving, double-interlock, weft-wrapping and weft-faced patterning techniques are all employed.

Khuzetstan Afshars (pl 23) are produced by descendants of the original Afshar tribesmen who settled in this region of south-west Iran in the 12th century. They are usually quite small, often rectangular, employ two or three medallions on an open or sparsely decorated field and use a limited palette of dark reds and blues, with hints of cream or white. They are woven predominantly in slitweave, although occasionally in double interlock.

Aimaq or Chahar Aimaq (pl 10) Name applied to four Farsi/Persian-speaking nomadic, semi-nomadic and sedentary tribes of mixed ethnic origin (Turkic, Mongolian, Persian and Arab) who inhabit a vast area in north-west and west central Afghanistan. ('Chahar' means four and 'Aimaq' is a Mongolian word for nomad.) The largest and most important weaving tribe is the Taimani, but the Firozkohi, Jamshidi and the settled Qala-i-Nau Hazaras also produce a number of interesting flatwoven items. (*See* Qala-i-Nau, p. 139)

Taimani (pl 10) are semi-nomads, divided into about a dozen main clans and several smaller sub-clans, who inhabit a vast area of west central Afghanistan. They are among the most prolific and important weavers in the region and are primarily responsible for the Afghan war rugs, as well as a huge range of kilims, pile rugs, *torbahs* and other artefacts. Taimani kilims are usually small to medium in size, woven in a number of techniques – including semi-pile, *soumak*, weft-wrapping and weft-faced patterning – and feature a variety of prayer-rug, pictorial and abstract geometric (often all-over repeating) designs. They are usually in the low price bracket, but exceptional items (including war rugs) may cost a little more.

Note Taimani weavings are often mistakenly classified as Belouch.

Firozkohi means 'mountains of turquoise' and is probably an oblique reference to the tribe's territorial origins. They are still predominantly semi-nomadic and most of their weaving is either for personal use or for the domestic market. Their kilims are usually long and narrow and they also produce *dasterkans*, *torbahs* and other artefacts – mainly in balanced plainweave, with embroidered geometric patterns in brown, orange, green, white and cherry red.

Jamshidi are now mainly sedentary farmers and traders (in and around Herat), but they still produce some essentially tribal items. These

War motifs found on Afghan war kilims. *From top left clockwise:* helicopter; tank; rifle; aeroplane

are very similar to Firozkohi weavings, but few find their way on to Western markets.

Arab weaving groups Pockets of Arab weavers are found throughout Iran, Afghanistan and other parts of the kilim-weaving region, but are not normally classified as Arab weaving groups because their kilims are far closer in character and appearance to other local items than to a homogeneous Arab style (*see* Firdous Belouch, p. 125). Authentic Arab tribal weaving is confined to North Africa where – although most Arab weavers are now settled, producing items that conform to the localized regional style – a few groups both retain a nomadic or semi-nomadic existence and also their specific tribal identity. (*See* Chapter IV)

Arab kilims are generally large and rectangular or long and narrow woven in slitweave and plainweave, brightly coloured and employ banded designs with repeating geometric (or *wasm*) infill motifs. They are not as common as Berber tribal weavings and are usually priced in the low-to-medium bracket. The most prolific Arab tribal weaving groups include:

The Chiadma, close neighbours of the Oulad Bou Sbaa, who generally use a mixture of weaving techniques (plainweave, slitweave and pile insertions) with a broader range of more intricate compositions. They are not dissimilar to some Iranian tribal weavings, but have brighter colours.

The Oulad Bou Sbaa, who live in the Tennsift region, near Casablanca in Morocco, and frequently employ banded compositions with relatively sparse infill decorations using mainly slitweave and plainweave techniques. Their palette is exceptionally warm and bright.

Bakhtiari A major sub-tribe of the Lurs – believed to be one of 30 tribes that migrated from Syria in the 14th century – who live primarily on either side of the Zagros Mountains, around the town of Shushtar and the Chahar Mahal Valley, in western Iran. They can be broken down into a number of separate clans or sub-tribes and, although many have now been assimilated into the settled population, some continue their nomadic way of life and produce authentic tribal flatweaves.

Bakhtiari kilims are generally long and narrow, woven in the double-interlock technique – which results in sturdy items with a stiff feel – and employ a wide variety of mainly geometric motifs in medallion, repeating and all-over formats, as well as more naturalistic *boteh* and

panelled designs. Colours are mainly confined to different shades of deep red, blue, reddish brown, yellow ochre, cream and white. Bags, animal trappings and artefacts are also made and most Bakhtiari weavings are normally in the low-to-medium price bracket. There are two main divisions of Bakhtiari weaving:

Chahar Mahal Bakhtiaris which are made in and around their summer pastures in the Chahar Mahal Valley. They usually use a wider range of small geometric and naturalistic motifs, e.g., *botehs* and tiny human and animal figures. They are often marketed in Shiraz.

Shushtar Bakhtiaris, which are marketed in the town of Shuster (near their winter quarters), and generally employ medallions and various rhomboid central motifs set against an open or sparsely decorated field. They are usually harder and stiffer than other Bakhtiaris.

Belouch (pls 19, 25, 26, 38) A mainly Indo-European tribal group of largely nomadic and semi-nomadic herdsmen who occupy a vast, inhospitable area stretching from eastern Iran through Afghanistan into western Pakistan. The exact origins of the Belouch (which simply means 'nomad' or 'wanderer') are unclear. We know that they were established in the region during the 11th and 12th centuries, but there is no evidence to say where they came from or why they came. Some of their folk myths claim descent from Nebuchadnezzar, King of Babylon, and it is quite possible that they migrated eastwards from Arabia or Aleppo (Syria). The more general belief is, however, that they were Persian nomads who fled eastwards into the more hostile regions of Baluchistan and the adjacent areas to the west and north in order to escape the Turkic invasions of the 11th century onwards. This view is supported by the fact that many of the major tribes are Farsi/Persian-speaking, but it fails to explain why other tribes (e.g., the Brahui) speak a Dravidian (south Indian) language and have incorporated several Indian customs into their otherwise orthodox Sunnite Muslim social and religious rites. It is possible, therefore, that the Belouch are a fusion of at least two migratory ethnic groups – one (Farsi-speaking) that moved eastwards from Persia and another (Dravidian-speaking) that travelled westwards from India. However, whatever major cultural differences may have existed have been largely eroded over the last 1,000 years and the Belouch can now be viewed as a relatively homogeneous tribal grouping that is among the most prolific and accomplished of all the authentic tribal weaving groups.

Belouch kilims, bags, animal trappings and other artefacts are produced by a number of sub-tribes and clans throughout eastern Iran, Afghanistan and western Pakistan. They are made using several techniques (weft wrapping, weft-faced patterning, weft twining, plainweave and supplementary pile insertion) – in almost every conceivable size and shape – and normally employ good quality wool. Their designs are equally varied and include numerous banded compositions (usually with intricate infill decorations), prayer rugs, all-over geometric (or occasionally stylized floral) motifs and pictorial rugs. The Belouch palette is generally rather sombre and often limited to interplays of different shades of red and blue with white and yellow highlights, although brighter and more varied colours are frequently used in pictorial items. Belouch kilims normally fall into the low price category (although exceptional items, especially pictorial or semi-pile may cost a little more) and are generally widely available on most Western markets. Each sub-tribe or regional division has its own particular variation on the general Belouch style – although, in practice, specific attributions are rarely made – and the following are the ones most commonly applied.
Note Taimani, Aimaq and Mushwani items are often marketed as Belouch.

Baluchistan Belouch are woven by nomadic, semi-nomadic and settled tribesmen living in the Province of Baluchistan, western Pakistan. They are usually more brightly coloured than most Belouch kilims – employing a basic palette of light red, orange, blue and white, frequently in banded designs that alternate bands of monochrome plainweave with intricately decorated (often in distinctive white fret or lace patterns) bands of weft-faced patterning or weft twining. They are normally in the low price category.

Charaknasur Belouch are made in the Charaknasur district of south-west Afghanistan and are similar to Farah weavings, although fewer prayer rugs are produced. They are generally considered to be among the finest of all Belouch items and usually fall into the low-to-medium price bracket.

Farah Belouch derive their name from the marketing town of Farah, in western Afghanistan, used by the Belouch of the region. They usually have an extremely dark palette (often dominated by black) with a very limited use of white or yellow highlights. Several basic compositions are employed, including prayer-rug designs. Large items are frequently made in two halves and then sewn together. Generally, Farah kilims are finely woven and fall into the low price bracket.

Firdous Belouch (pl 38) are woven by ethnic Arabs who live in and around the town of Firdous in the Khorassan Province of Iran. They are similar to Belouch (and often Kurdish) items woven in the region and normally fall into the low-to-medium price bracket.

Herat Belouch is a generic name – derived from the city of Herat, in western Afghanistan – that is often applied to any Belouch kilim made in the country.

Malaki Belouch (pl 26) refers to a style of kilim produced by nomads who inhabit the vast Dasht-i-Margo (Desert of Death) in south-western Afghanistan. They employ a mixture of weaving techniques (including semi-pile), a palette of dark reds, blues and black, highlighted with white, cream and pale yellow, and a variety of mainly banded and prayer-rug designs. They are sometimes decorated with glass beads and cowrie shells. Malaki kilims are considered by some authorities to be among the finest of all Belouch weavings and usually retail within the low-to-medium price bracket.

Maldari Belouch are produced by the Maldari (meaning sheep or goat owner) sub-tribe, who inhabit western Afghanistan and are arguably the most primitive of all the Belouch weaving groups. Maldari kilims have a similar range of designs, colours and weaving techniques to other Belouch items, but their execution is usually slightly simpler and cruder. They are nevertheless attractive and collectable, and are among the cheapest Belouch kilims.

Meshed Belouch is a generic name – derived from the town of Meshed, in eastern Iran, where the Belouch of the region have traditionally marketed their wares – that is often applied to certain Iranian Belouch items. Banded compositions and all-over designs, with slightly brighter colours, are common and they are generally considered to be among the finer and slightly more expensive Belouch kilims.

Nisaphur Belouch (pl 25) derive their name from a marketing town in north-east Iran associated with extremely finely made items that often feature fairly naturalistic depictions of people, animals and birds – either in pictorial or 'all-over' folk-art designs.

Berber weaving groups (pl 17) Most authentic tribal weaving in North Africa is produced by Berbers living a nomadic, semi-nomadic or settled life in the Tennsift coastal region and the High and Middle Atlas Mountain ranges in Morocco. Several individual tribes, each with their own repertoire of designs, weave primarily for personal use or to sell in the local souks and only a few of the larger and tribal groups provide a significant number of items for the Western market. (*See* Berbers, p. 49)

Berber kilims are generally woven in a mixture of plainweave and weft-faced patterning, and feature a wide variety of banded and, less frequently, geometric repeating designs. The colour schemes range from very dark (reds, purple, black and blue, with white and yellow highlights) to much brighter interplays of pale red, orange, yellow ochre, white and blue. Middle Atlas and Tennsift tribal weavings are produced by mainly nomadic and semi-nomadic tribes. In contrast, most of the major High Atlas weaving groups – although tribal in character – are village or regionally based. Most Berber kilims are in the low price bracket. (*See* Regional and workshop weaving groups, Azrou, Boujaad, Glaoua, Hanbel, Oudzem, Taznakht and Klenifra)

Middle Atlas tribal weavings include:

Beni M'Guild kilims which are usually large and rectangular, with intensely decorated bands and square compartments, in a dark palette of blue, black and red contrasted by white highlights and outlines. Beni M'Tir kilims are similar, but frequently contain all-over repeating diamond motifs.

Beni Quarain kilims which are predominantly rectangular, small to medium in size, often featuring banded designs of alternating monochrome plainweave and highly decorated weft-faced patterning in a sharply contrasting palette of light and dark colours.

Zair kilims (pl 17) which are very similar in colour and design to Zaiane items, but slightly 'wilder' in appearance – often featuring rows of tiny metallic or bead decorations, and tassels extruding from the face of the kilim.

Tennsift tribal weavings include:

Zaiane kilims which are woven in a variety of sizes, using a dark palette (red, blue, purple and some white) and often feature alternating bands of broad, intensely decorated sections separated by narrow monochrome strips.

Zemmour kilims which are mainly large and rectangular (although some smaller items are made) and are very similar to Zaiane kilims, but with a brighter palette – often based on a pale red ground. The Zemmour tribe is one of the most prolific Berber weaving groups.

Karakalpaks Turkic-speaking people – closely related to the Kazakhs, but believed to contain people of Bulgarian ancestry – who inhabit the former Tartar ASSR (ancient Tartary) and other parts of Central Asia, especially Uzbekistan. They are sometimes referred to as Tartars.

Karakalpak kilims frequently employ an octagonal (or elephant's foot) *gul* that is very similar to the one associated with Afghan rugs. They generally resemble Uzbek weavings, but are not usually as finely woven or produced in the same range of designs. Bags, animal trappings and artefacts are also made, and most Karakalpak items are in the low-to-medium price bracket.

Kazakhs Turkic-speaking people of Mongol appearance, believed to be an amalgamation of the Kipchak Turkic tribesmen, who migrated to Transoxiana in the 8th century, and Mongol invaders who settled in the area during the 13th century. The Kazakhs believe that they are descended from the three sons of a single progenitor, who divided the nation into three Hordes or *Ordas*, each controlling the eastern (Great), central (Central) and western (Little) regions of what is now Kazakhstan. Today, the vast majority of ethnic Kazakhs live in Kazakhstan, the Sinkiang Province in China and Mongolia, but can also be found in other parts of the weaving region.

Note Kazakh is also a town in former Soviet Azerbaijan which lends its name to one of the traditional Caucasian weaving groups. (*See* Traditional Caucasian weaving groups, p. 115)

Kazakh kilims do not employ *guls* as their main decorative motif, but are otherwise very similar to other central Asian Turkic weavings. They are generally well made, using the standard Turkoman palette of deep red and dark blue with yellow ochre, orange and white traceries and highlights, in a range of repeating and all-over formats based around diamond and hooked geometric forms. Bags, animal

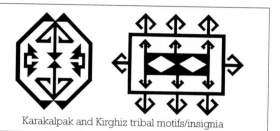

Karakalpak and Kirghiz tribal motifs/insignia

trappings and artefacts are also made and most Kazakh weavings lean towards the middle price bracket.

Khamseh or Khamsa A Persian word meaning 'five' that is used to describe a confederation of five tribes of different, mainly Turkic, Arab and Luri ethnic origins who now live in the Fars province of south-west Iran. The Khamseh – like the Shahsavan – are essentially a political group, created in 1862 by the Qavam family (who were rich merchants in the town of Shiraz) to guard their trade routes against Qashga'i raids. Many Khamseh tribesmen are now settled, although some still retain their nomadic way of life. The kilims produced by each of the five tribes (the Ainallu, the Baharlu, the Bassira, the Jabbareh and the Sheibari) – despite being slightly different in character and appearance, and regardless of whether they are of nomadic or village origin – are usually marketed under the collective heading of Khamsehs.

Note The Khamseh tribal confederation is not to be confused with the Khamseh district in north-west Iran – which derives its name from the five rivers in the region and the former districts they defined. It is inhabited by the Shahsavan.

Khamseh kilims are generally rectangular, ranging in size from small to large, and woven using slitweave and double-interlock techniques. A number of bags, animal trappings and artefacts are also produced. Designs vary considerably – partly reflecting their diverse ethnic make-up and partly influenced by Afshar and, to a lesser extent, Qashga'i weavings. Khamseh kilims are usually less colourful than those woven by their more illustrious neighbours, but are otherwise sufficiently similar to make precise attribution extremely difficult. They fall into the low-to-medium price bracket and are sometimes sold under the general classifications of Fars or Shiraz (their principal marketing town).

Kirghiz Turkic-speaking people whose exact origins are obscure, but they are believed to be connected to the Turanian Turks (or Tartars) who inhabit the Steppe country of southern Siberia and northern Mongolia. Today, most Kirghiz live in the Kirghizstan Republic, but there are also settlements in the Sinkiang Province in China and other former Soviet Central Asian Republics.

Kirghiz kilims have a close affinity with items from the Sinkiang Province of China, employing a similar palette of muted reds, blues, yellow and orange ochres, highlighted with darker blues and white. Their designs rely on repeating, all-over and panelled formats, based around a variety of geometric and naturalistic (usually floral) motifs. Bags, animal trappings and artefacts are also produced. Kirghiz items are generally very well made and fall into the medium price bracket.

Kurds (pls 24, 32) Indo-European people who are among the oldest inhabitants of the Iranian plateau and the vaguely defined geographical area that is generally referred to as ethnic Kurdistan. Their exact origins are obscure. A tribe called the Kuti (or Guti) were known to have existed in ancient Assyria and Babylonia (Iraq, Syria, Palestine and south-eastern Turkey) as early as the 2nd millennium BC and later Assyrian documents (c. 900–600 BC) refer first to the 'Kurtie' and then to the 'Kardu'. Kurdish folklore traces their origins to one of King Solomon's 500 *jinns* or genies (magical beings who can be controlled by mortals) who was dispatched to find 500 virgins for Solomon's harem, but, failing to return before Solomon died, settled in the Zagros Mountains (in southern Iran) with his virgin bride and fathered the Kurdish race. Taken as an allegory, this reinforces the belief that the Kurds originated in Palestine and Syria and then migrated to the north and east. However, it wasn't until around AD 640 that the name 'Kurd' was first used to describe a number of tribes and tribal groupings in west Persia and the southern Caucasus.

In the 16th century the Kurds formed an alliance with the Armenians (with whom they share a common history of maintaining their cultural and political identity despite centuries of conflict, subjugation, persecution and forced migration), after being transported to the Caucasus by the Turks in an attempt to push these two troublesome groups into mutual conflict. This resulted in the Turks being driven out. Today, the majority of Kurds continue to live in ethnic Kurdistan and, mainly as a legacy of forced transportation by a succession of Turkish and Persian rulers, there are also large Kurdish concentrations in the Iranian provinces of Azerbaijan and Khorassan and more isolated pockets throughout other parts of Iran, Turkey, the Caucasus and the Middle East. Most Kurds are now settled in towns and villages, but some still retain a nomadic or semi-nomadic way of life and contemporary Kurdish weaving runs the gamut of tribal and regional items – from the primitive charm of nomadic bags and horse blankets to the precision and sophistication of Senneh regional kilims.

Kurdish kilims are so diverse – both in their areas of production, and in their overall character and appearance – that it is impossible to classify all the items woven by ethnic Kurds into a homogeneous Kurdish weaving group. However, some dealers not only attempt to unify all Kurdish weaving, but also often classify almost any attractive item of uncertain attribution, originating from eastern Turkey or western Iran, as Kurdish. Similarly, regional kilims made in the towns of Bidjar and Senneh, in Kurdistan, are undoubtedly woven by a predominantly Kurdish workforce, but it is doubtful whether these items can be considered 'Kurdish' in the sense that they are characteristic of a homogeneous tribal group. In reality, the only factors that unify Kurdish kilims are they are generally well made (usually employing slitweave, with the occasional use of supplementary weft wrapping or weft insertion techniques); employ a rich and well-balanced palette of reds, blues, orange, brown and yellow ochres, with the supplementary use of green, cream and white; and are usually produced in attractive and harmonious designs, regardless of their sophistication or simplicity. A number of nomadic or semi-nomadic Kurdish tribes still exist, but very few of the kilims they produce can be traced back to a specific source. In general, Kurdish weaving is classified according to the towns or regions where they live or market their wares. (*See* Regional and workshop weaving groups: Bidjar, Senneh, Van)

Kutchis Itinerant tinkers and traders of Indo-European origin, who wander with their caravans and camels throughout eastern, central and southern Afghanistan. They have been dubbed the 'gypsies' of Central Asia. The word 'Kutchi' is often used by other inhabitants of the region as a term of derision, implying that something or someone is shoddy, worthless or not to be trusted, and seems to reflect the general view of the Kutchis as a people, rather than being an objective comment on their weaving skills.

Kutchi kilims are usually long and narrow, woven in a loose slitweave technique, and feature a variety of medallion and repeating geometric designs – often embellished with glass beads, small coins, pieces of metal and synthetic threads. The colours are generally bright, dominated by red, orange, reddish browns, yellow ochres and white, and perfectly complement the primitive, rough-hewn character of the composition and weave. They normally fall into the low price bracket and are sometimes known as Mukkurs, after their marketing town in southern Afghanistan.

Lurs (pl 28) Indo-European tribal people, believed to be among the earliest inhabitants of south-west Iran, who have largely retained their nomadic and pastoral lifestyle. Very little is known about Luri history except that they came to prominence in the 8th century BC, as part of the Elamite Kingdom (which extended eastwards from Babylon to the Zagros Mountains) and went on to produce the famous Luristan bronzes. They were divided for some of their history into 'the Great Lurs' (who lived in the south) and 'the Little Lurs' (who occupied the northern territories), but, by the 15th century, this division had disappeared. They are now viewed as one homogeneous tribal and ethnic group that contains a number of sub-tribes – the most important of which is the Bakhtiari. Today, the Lurs still live predominantly in their traditional territories, which stretch from the Iran–Iraq border in the west, through Luristan and southern Kurdistan, across the Zagros Mountains into the Fars province of southern Iran. They speak a language closely related to Farsi (Persian) and are sometimes referred to as the 'Kuhi', which simply means 'mountain people' – presumably because of the rugged, mountainous region in which they have lived for at least 3,000 years.

Luri kilims are very similar in design, colour and weave to those woven by the Qashga'i and, although generally less colourful and intricately decorated, many Luri items have been wrongly attributed to their more fashionable neighbours. It is impossible to say with any degree of certainty who copied from whom, but the relative histories of the two groups suggest that the Qashga'i developed and refined a number of basic Luri designs. Luri kilims are made in a variety of sizes, mainly rectangular, and fall into the low and low-to-medium price brackets.

Mushwani Farsi-speaking semi-nomadic and settled tribesmen of Indo-European – probably Pathan – ancestry, who inhabit the Herat and Badghis provinces of western Afghanistan. Splinter groups may, however, be found elsewhere in the region. They are often bracketed with the Belouch or the Aimaq because of the similarities in their lifestyles, location and weaving.

Mushwani kilims are usually small to medium in size, rectangular or long and narrow, and feature a wide range of designs, similar to those favoured by Belouch and Aimaq weavers. The Mushwani palette is even darker than that of the Belouch, frequently including a dominant field colour of black or blue-black highlighted by dark red, deep yellow ochre, brown or a slightly paler shade of blue. This extremely sombre colour scheme often features in a distinctive Mushwani composition based on concentric hooked diamonds expanding outwards across the entire field. Mushwani kilims are well made and fall into the low-to-medium price bracket.

Qashga'i or Kashgay (pls 15, 36) Nomadic, semi-nomadic and settled tribesmen of Turkic origin who live primarily in the Fars province of south-west Iran. Their exact origins are obscure – some historians trace their ancestry to the Mongol-Turkic army of Genghis Khan that overran Persia during the 13th century; others argue that they were part of the Seljuk Turkic invasion in the 11th century. There are also suggestions that they arrived much earlier, possibly as part of a Hephthalite (White Hun) incursion during the 5th or 6th century. What we do know is that after Genghis Khan's death, the conquered territories were divided between his children and grandchildren, who founded Mongol-Turkic khanates (*see* Chapter IV). Some of the occupying armies stayed on and were later joined by other Mongol-Turkic migrants who brought with them their weaving traditions and skills.

The Qashga'i themselves claim to have originated in Kashgaria (East Turkestan), although their name may also have derived from a famous tribal leader, Jani Agha Qashga'i, who exercised authority over the tribes of the Fars province during the Safavid era. Regardless of their origins, the Qashga'i have long been among the finest and most prolific of all tribal weaving groups.

Qashga'i kilims are produced in a wide variety of medallion, repeating, all-over, panelled and banded designs – usually with an array of tiny geometric, floral, animal, birds and human forms scattered, apparently at random, across the field and within the main elements of the design. The compositions are usually geometric in essence, but the vibrancy of the Qashga'i palette (with its full range of primary and ochred shades), coupled with the folk-art quality of many of the infill motifs, give many Qashga'i kilims an almost naturalistic feel. However, the quality of Qashga'i kilims varies considerably and a number of items sold as Qashga'i are possibly either Luri or Khamseh in origin or produced (in Qashga'i designs) in commercial workshops in the marketing town of Shiraz. Bags, animal trappings and artefacts are also woven. Authentic tribal Qashga'is range between the low-medium to medium price bracket. (*See* Lurs, p. 128, and Shiraz, p. 141)

Shahsavan (pls 2, 16) A tribal confederation composed mainly of ethnic Turkic, Kurdish, Tadjik and Georgian nomads and semi-nomads who inhabit several areas of Iran. Their name means 'those who are loyal to the Shah' and they were formed by Shah Abbas, at the beginning of the 17th century, as a buffer against the rebellious Kyzylbash (Dervish) movement. However, several Shahsavan tribes maintained the confederation after the Kyzylbash threat receded. Today, some Shahsavan tribesmen have settled among the Bakhtiari (near the Zagros Mountains in the south-west) and other tribal groups in the Fars and Khorassan provinces (in the south and east), but most still live their traditional lifestyle in a broad area, stretching from the town of Veramin (just south of Tehran) to the north Azerbaijan border in the north-west of the country.

Shahsavan kilims are among the most attractive, vibrant and diverse of all Iranian tribal weavings. The designs range from simple banded schemes to extremely intricate 'Caucasian-inspired' repeating and medallion compositions. Stylized animals and birds (especially camels, deer and horses), floral and human forms, and a wide variety of – often hooked or crenellated – geometric and symbolic motifs are often employed, both as major compositional elements and additional infill decorations. The Shahsavan palette is generally a subtle combination of vibrant primary colours (mainly reds, blues and greens) balanced by more subdued shades of yellow and orange ochre, cream and brown. Their kilims are usually long and narrow – although some rectangular items are produced – and woven in basic slitweave enhanced by a variety of supplementary weaving techniques; a wide range of *jajims*, *vernehs*, *soufrehs*, *rukorssis*, bags, animal trappings and artefacts are also made. Most Shahsavan items fall into the low-to-medium and medium price brackets. The Shahsavan are composed of a number of sub-tribes or tribal groupings normally classified according to their region or major marketing town.

Bidjar Shahsavan kilims are woven primarily by settled tribesmen living in a number of small villages around the town of Bidjar, in Kurdistan. They are very similar to those woven in Mogan, but tend to employ a lighter palette of orange and reddish orange, yellow, blue, light brown and pink.

Hastrud Shahsavan kilims are made by nomadic, semi-nomadic and settled tribesmen, who either live in or spend the winter in and around the north-western town of Hastrud. These kilims are more loosely woven (in slitweave) than most other Shahsavan items as they usually employ banded designs – often with Caucasian or Turkic infill motifs – or large hooked or crenellated medallions in a slightly pastel palette of reds, blues, greens, pink and brown, although darker shades are also found.

Khamseh Shahsavan kilims are produced by mainly settled and, to a lesser extent, semi-nomadic tribesmen, living in and around the northern Iranian district of Khamseh, which contains the five former districts of Zanjan. They are very similar to Mogan kilims, but have a darker palette of red, blue, brown and yellow ochre.

Note The Khamseh district is not to be confused with the Khamseh tribe of the Fars Province in southern Iran.

Mianeh Shahsavan kilims are made by nomadic, semi-nomadic and settled tribesmen, who either live or winter in and around the town of Mianeh. They are usually larger and more rectangular than items made in the nearby town of Hastrud and feature a similar range of designs, which are often more finely articulated by the use of supplementary weft-wrapped contour lines, and employ a deeper, brighter palette of mainly red, orange, yellow and blue.

Mogan Shahsavan kilims (pl 2) are produced by mainly nomadic and semi-nomadic tribesmen who inhabit the Mogan Plain in the north-east corner of the Iranian Province of Azerbaijan, bordering the Azerbaijan Republic, which is considered to be their traditional homeland. Mogan kilims are generally seen as the most 'tribally' authentic of all Shahsavan weavings. They are tightly woven in a variety of mainly banded designs – either based on alternating bands of monochrome plainweave or 'Caucasian-inspired' repeating infill motifs (mainly star and spider/tarantula) – and employ a darker, richer palette of predominantly reds, blues, greens, browns, yellow and white than most other Shahsavan groups. Mogan kilims are usually long and narrow, sometimes woven in two pieces and then sewn together. A variety of bags, animal trappings, artefacts and other weavings, often featuring stylized animal, bird and floral repeating or all-over designs, are also produced.

Qazvin Shahsavan kilims are produced by mainly settled and semi-nomadic tribesmen living in and around the town of Qazvin, in northern Iran. They are usually long and narrow, woven in fine slitweave, with supplementary dovetailing, and feature a wide range of Shahsavan and occasionally other tribal designs. The palette is generally more subdued than usual, but often contains relatively bright turmeric yellow – distinguishing Qazvin kilims from other Shahsavan work.

Saveh Shahsavan kilims are woven by nomadic, semi-nomadic and settled tribesmen, who inhabit the town of Saveh and the surrounding area in north central Iran. They are similar to Qazvin kilims, but are generally stiffer and more coarsely woven, often on cotton warps.

Veramin Shahsavan kilims are woven by nomadic, semi-nomadic and settled tribesmen, who inhabit the area and villages around the town of Veramin. They are generally well made, using a variety of weaving techniques, in a wide range of colours and designs – especially traditional north-west Iranian banded compositions, often with rosette or 'S' pattern infill decorations – and are frequently rectangular in shape. Veramin is a major kilim-weaving centre, inhabited by other tribal groups (mainly Afshars, Lurs and Kurds), who have had a reciprocal influence on Shahsavan weaving – often making it extremely difficult to pin-point the exact tribal attribution for items from this region.

Tadjiks Turkic tribesmen who speak Tadjik, a variant of Persian, and are believed to be descendants of Persian, Arab and Turkic people. They now live predominantly in the former Soviet Tadjik Republic and Afghanistan. They are not generally considered to be a significant weaving group and Tadjik kilims rarely, if ever, find their way on to Western markets. However, ethnic Tadjik weavers form part of the Shahsavan and other weaving groups.

Tartars (Tartari) Turkic-speaking tribesmen whose name has become synonymous with intractability and ferocity, and whose habit of tenderizing meat by putting it under their saddles and then eating it raw is the inspiration behind the culinary dish Steak Tartar. The Tartars are believed to have descended from indigenous Turkic tribes of the Kipchak group, with Mongol and Bulgarian elements, and once inhabited a vast region stretching from the Crimean Peninsula, through the middle Volga Valley, the Steppe country, southern Siberia and northern Mongolia. Today, the majority of Tartars live in the former Soviet Tartar and Uzbek Republics. In conjunction with the Kirghiz, Yakut and other more Mongoloid Turkic tribes, they are sometimes referred to as the Turanian Turks.

Tartari kilims (pl 27), as defined by most dealers, is a misleading, generic term used to describe items woven, mainly in Afghanistan, by Uzbek and other Turkic weavers, which conform to the following two specific styles:

Ranghi (or red) kilims are usually large and rectangular, finely woven in double interlock and composed of variations of an all-over diamond grid, inwardly decorated with repeating Turkic motifs, set against a deep red field with blue, yellow, green and white outlines.

Safid (or white) kilims (pl 27) are generally long and narrow, finely woven using weft-faced plainweave and weft-faced patterning and employ a specific banded composition in which narrow, widely spaced bands of colour (usually inwardly decorated with zig-zag and other Turkic motifs) are set against a monochrome white or cream field. They are closely associated with the Afghan town of Sar-i-Pul.

Timuri Nomadic and semi-nomadic tribesmen of uncertain origins who inhabit similar territories to the Belouch and Aimaq. Timuri kilims are almost indistinguishable from Belouch and Aimaq items and are usually marketed as such.

Turkomen (pls 18, 20) Eastern Turks belonging to the south-western branch of the Turkic language group, who were almost exclusively nomadic until the early 20th century, and who now live – either a nomadic, semi-nomadic or settled lifestyle – mainly in the Turkmenistan Republic and other former Central Asian Republics. Pockets of Turkomen can also be found in Afghanistan, Iran, Turkey, Iraq and Syria. The Turkomen are divided into a number of major tribal groups (e.g., the Ersari, Tekke), each of which has a number of sub or associated tribes (e.g., Arabatchi, Beshir). However, dealers sometimes mistakenly classify items produced by the Karakalpaks, Kazakhs, Kirghiz, Uzbeks and Uighurs as Turkoman weavings.

Turkoman kilims are generally based on all-over, repeating *gul* designs, with each individual tribe and major sub-tribe having its own distinctive *gul* and normally employ a palette restricted to various shades of red, offset by dark blue, white and yellow outlining and highlights. However, other geometric forms sometimes feature, either in repeating or banded formats, and a few additional colours (mainly brown, deep yellow and cream or white) may also be used. A number of individual tribes are either no longer significant producers of kilims or their individuality has been absorbed into a more general regional style. However, the following need to be considered as separate weaving groups.

Ersari kilims, although still woven in Turkmenistan and Uzbekistan, are mainly produced today in Afghanistan and have become synonymous with Afghan weaving to the point where they are often referred to simply as Afghans. Many Ersari tribesmen have now settled in villages and towns throughout Afghanistan and are responsible for much of the country's regional and workshop weaving. However, some have retained their tribal traditions and continue to produce classic Ersari kilims – in both *gul* and other repeating formats. The Arabatchi, Beshir, Charchangi, Jangalrik and Kizyl Azak weavers are generally considered to be either sub-tribes or otherwise connected to the Ersari weaving group. (*See* Labijar, p. 138)

Saryk or Sarukh kilims are produced mainly in Turkmenistan and to a lesser extent Afghanistan; they are very similar to Ersari items, although generally more finely woven. The Saryk are closely associated with the Salor (considered to be the finest of all Turkoman weavers until the beginning of the 20th century when their production declined) and weave items that employ close variants on the Salor *gul*, in addition to a range of their own more distinctive *guls*.

Tekke kilims are produced predominantly in Turkmenistan, but also in northern Iran and parts of Central Asia. They are very similar to Saryk and Yomut items, and are usually considered to be the model for generic Bokhara rugs woven in workshops throughout Soviet Central Asia and Pakistan.

Yomut or Yomud kilims (pls 18, 20) are made in Turkmenistan, Afghanistan and to a lesser extent northern Iran. They are like other Turkoman items, but generally use a wider variety of repeating geometric motifs, in addition to traditional *guls*.

Uighurs Turkic-speaking tribesmen who inhabit ancient East Turkestan (now the Sinkiang Province in China) and also, to a lesser degree, other parts of Central Asia. They are believed to be of Turko-Mongol descent and closely related to the Uzbeks. Although the Uighurs share a common heritage with the other Turkic peoples, their close proximity to the Chinese sphere of influence has tempered their religious, cultural and artistic expression.

Uighur kilims possess a fusion of Islamic and Chinese artistic expression. They are usually of good quality, woven in slitweave and employ slight variations on traditional Turkoman designs, predominantly in a more pastel 'Chinese' palette. Uighur kilims are often marketed as Kashgaria, Kashgar or East Turkestan items, and occasionally after the principle towns in the region – i.e., Khotan, Yarkand or Kansu.

Uzbeks (pl 42) Turkic-speaking people of Turko-Mongol descent, thought to be a sub-tribe or breakaway group of the Uighur and Turkomen tribes who migrated from East Turkestan to the area known as the Golden Horde sometime during the early part of the 1st millennium. Their name was derived from their leader, Uzbek Khan (r. *c*. 1313–40), who converted them to Islam. 'Uzbek' became the collective term for the Muslim section of Genghis Khan's Golden Horde. Today, the majority of Uzbeks live in the Uzbekistan Republic, but significant numbers also inhabit Afghanistan and other parts of Central Asia.

Uzbek kilims are arguably the most varied in both colour and design of all the items made by Turkic weaving groups. They range from Turkoman-style *gul* designs to a variety of banded, panelled, zig-zag, prayer-rug, all-over geometric and stylized floral compositions. The Uzbek palette is usually dominated by various shades of red, with dark blue, brown and yellow ochre, and white secondary colours, but items with white, cream or brown grounds are also produced. Uzbek weaving techniques are equally diverse and include a substantial number of *ghudjeri*, *suzani* and

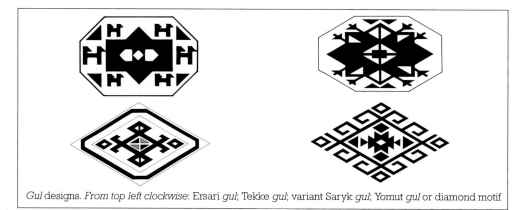

Gul designs. *From top left clockwise*: Ersari *gul*; Tekke *gul*; variant Saryk *gul*; Yomut *gul* or diamond motif

ikats, as well as various bags, animal trappings and artefacts. Most Uzbek weaving falls into the low-to-medium price bracket, although finer items may be slightly more expensive. In addition to tribal items, Uzbek weavers are also extremely influential in a number of Afghan regional weaving groups. (*See* Sar-i-Pul, p. 140, Maimana, p. 138, and Tartars, p. 131)

Yuruks Nomadic and semi-nomadic tribesmen who inhabit the Yuncu and Taurus Mountain regions of western and southern Turkey. The term 'Yuruk' is derived from a Turkic word, meaning 'nomad' or 'those who wander', and has no specific ethnic connotation. However, the vast majority of Yuruk tribesmen are direct descendants of the Turko-Mongol people (closely related to the Hungarians, Finns and Samoyeds), who migrated southwards during the 6th century AD and later occupied most of Turkey, Central Asia and eastern China. Most of these original migrants were gradually absorbed – during the subsequent Turkic and Mongol invasions – into the general Turkish population and eventually adopted a more sedentary way of life, but a few have consistently retained their nomadic lifestyle. In the 9th century they were referred to as 'Turkomen' and later (during the Ottoman Empire) came to be known as the 'Yuruks'. The terms *gocebe* and *yerli* are used respectively to describe the tribes that lead nomadic and semi-nomadic lifestyles.

Yuruk kilims are produced in a number of designs – mainly banded and all-over – which often feature interlocking *perepedil* (ram's horn) and other geometric or symbolic motifs – and employ a limited palette of predominantly dark reds and blues. They are usually quite finely woven, in slitweave, with varying amounts of goat and horse hair. *Cuvals* are also produced, normally in plainweave with supplementary weft wrapping.

Taurus Yuruk kilims may be marketed as Yuruks or Taurus Yuruks, but are often sold as Muts (after the major marketing town in the region). Alternatively, they are sometimes referred to as *Dag* (or mountain) kilims, although this term is often reserved for items featuring a square medallion with hooked corners, known as the 'bull's head motifs'.

Yuncu Yuruk kilims are usually marketed as Yuruks or Yuncu Yuruks, but may sometimes be sold as Baliksers because of their frequent similarity in colour and design to items woven in the main marketing town.

Regional and workshop weaving groups

This section concentrates on those weaving groups that produce items that conform to an identifiable uniformity of character and appearance. Contemporary workshops that make items in a range of styles not associated with their place of origin (e.g., Izmir and a number of other weaving centres in Turkey) are not included in this section, but a general description of the quality and appearance of these items can be found in Chapter VI.

The same weaving group (e.g., Bergama) sometimes produces both anonymous workshop items and their own distinctive regional ones. In such cases, separate descriptions have been included of both types of kilim.

Other weaving groups produce items in relatively sophisticated workshops that are aimed primarily at the export market, but still retain their traditional character and appearance (e.g., Senneh); or alternatively make regional items that are strongly influenced by the character and appearance of a specific – usually local – tribal group or groups (Shiraz). They will be referred to as regional/workshop and regional/tribal weaving groups respectively.

Adana Major town in southern Turkey that was the site of a 2nd-century BC Hittite settlement. It is now a major industrial and agricultural centre. However, many villages in the area still produce regional kilims, which are generally woven in slitweave; employ a bright palette of mainly reds, pink, orange and white; and feature a variety of medallion, prayer-rug and repeating designs; often with *elibelinde*, tree-of-life and bird motifs. Adana kilims are normally rectangular, produced in a variety of sizes, and fall into the low-to-medium price bracket. *Juvals*, *zillis* and *cicims* are also made.

Afyon Town in western Turkey that was a major centre for opium production ('Afyon' is Turkish for opium and the town's previous name, Afyonkarahisar, translates as 'dark opium castle'). It is also renowned for its distinctive kilims that often feature *parmalki* or finger motifs in a variety of medallion, all-over and prayer-rug formats. The Afyon palette ranges from light to garish – particularly in its use of apricot, blue, green, pink and yellow. Most items are woven, either in slitweave or plainweave, in a wide range of mainly rectangular sizes and fall into the low-to-medium price bracket.

Aksaray (pl 31) Agricultural town in central Turkey that produces good quality kilims that are very similar to those woven in Konya.

Antalya Major port on the Mediterranean coast of Turkey, founded in 200 BC by the King of Pergamum, Attalus II, which is now an important centre for the production of regional kilims made in a number of surrounding villages. Modern Antalya kilims are often fairly coarsely woven, usually in slitweave or plainweave (with occasional supplementary weft wrapping), and generally feature designs based on interlocking hexagonal medallions and repeating (often small) geometric motifs in a variety of rather light colours. Sizes range from small to large, usually rectangular, and most items fall into the low price bracket. Older items are generally more finely woven and expensive.

Ardebil (pl 6) Town in the Azerbaijan Province of north-west Iran that produces medium quality regional/tribal kilims for the domestic and export markets. Designs vary, but are usually based on a variety of typical north-west Iranian compositions – mainly repeating geometric motifs, zig-zag patterns and pole medallions. The colour schemes are frequently either subdued or extremely bright (sometimes garish), with a predominance of red, yellow ochre, orange, blue and green. They are normally woven in slitweave, sometimes with cotton warps, in a variety of sizes and shapes, and fall into the low price bracket.

Aydin Town near the Aegean coast in Turkey that produces good quality, mainly rectangular, regional kilims – invariably woven in slitweave, featuring a number of mainly prayer-rug, medallion and repeating geometric designs. The Aydin palette is generally bright and varied, and larger items are frequently woven in two halves. They are usually in the low-to-medium price bracket.

Azerbaijan Province in north-west Iran, bordering the Azerbaijan Republic, that is occupied by a large percentage of ethnic Azerbaijanis, as well as other Iranian tribal and ethnic groups. The term 'Azerbaijani' could legitimately be applied to any item woven in the region, but it is normally reserved for kilims made in the Caucasian Azerbaijan style, usually by ethnic Azerbaijanis. These items are frequently long and narrow, finely woven in slitweave, *soumak* and other supplementary

weft-patterning and weft-insertion techniques; feature pole medallions or other heraldic geometric motifs; and employ a palette of generally dark or sombre reds and blues. They range in price between low-to-medium and medium brackets. Kilims produced by other tribal weaving groups (Afshar, Shahsavan, etc.) or regional weaving groups (Ardebil, etc.) are normally marketed under their names. Unattributed items – not in the Azerbaijani style – are usually marketed as north-west Iranian, rather than Azerbaijan kilims.

Azrou (pl 7) Woven by Berber tribesmen who live in and around the Middle Atlas village of Azrou in Morocco. They are very similar to Zaiane kilims, but feature large areas of white in their banded designs.

Balikesir Town in western Turkey noted for good quality regional kilims – woven in slitweave or plainweave, with occasional supplementary weft wrapping – that employ designs based on an open or sparsely decorated field – generally known as 'empty field' kilims. They are more reminiscent of some Iranian tribal weavings (e.g., Luri, Shahsavan) than other Turkish regional items and are mainly woven for the domestic market and fall into the low-to-medium price range. Yuncu Yoruk kilims are sometimes marketed in the town and may be sold as Balikesirs.

Bergama (pl 11) City in western Turkey, near the site of the pre-Roman urban civilization of Pergamum, that is now one of the major centres for contemporary workshop kilims as well as producing its own distinctive regional items.

Bergama workshop kilims (pl 11) are generally rectangular, small to medium in size – woven in slitweave or plainweave, supplementary weft wrapping – and feature a wide range of traditional Turkish designs (especially 'hand of Fatima' and other small motifs in repeating or banded formats). Some essentially European – including Scandinavian 'folk-art' – compositions are also produced. Colour schemes range from traditional reds, blues, greens and yellows to more subdued pastel shades aimed at satisfying Western decorative tastes. Bergama workshop kilims are produced in standard and superior grades (the former falling into the low price bracket and the latter into the medium). A substantial number of contemporary workshop items are woven in the nearby village of Kozak and may be marketed under that name.

Bergama regional kilims are occasionally produced, in traditional colours and designs – mainly hand of Fatima – but are often indistinguishable from good quality workshop items of a similar appearance. A number of *zillis*, *cicims* and *juvals* are also made and some older items still find their way on to the market.

Bidjar (pl 34) Town in Kurdistan (Iran) noted for its extremely fine and hard-wearing pile rugs, but also a centre for the production of good quality regional kilims. Designs often feature a central medallion, which may be geometric or floral, set against an open or sparsely decorated field; frequently with intricately patterned borders, sometimes with human or animal figures. Colours vary, but are usually strong and employed in relatively sharp contrast, although they are rarely garish or disharmonious. The strongest design influence is Kurdish, but the effects of Shahsavan and other tribal and regional compositions are also evident. Bidjar kilims are normally woven in slitweave, sometimes with cotton warps; they are mainly long and narrow or rectangular, and fall into the low-to-medium or medium price brackets.

Boujaad Village in the High Atlas Mountains, near Marrakesh in Morocco, inhabited by Berber tribesmen. These kilims are similar to Zair kilims, but contain even more eccentric design features – including sewn-on metallic decorations, beads, synthetic fibres and other supplementary ornamentations.

Cal Small town, near Denizli in western Turkey, that produces decent quality, slitwoven kilims in a variety of mainly medallion designs, which are often set against an open or sparsely decorated field. Cal kilims are distinguished by their warm, rustic palette of mainly orange, red, pink, yellow ochre and green. They are usually rectangular, small to medium in size, and priced within the low-to-medium range.

Corum Town and region in northern Turkey that makes good quality kilims, woven in slitweave (often in two halves). They are noted for employing panelled or compartmentalized designs, inwardly decorated with a variety of small geometric and symbolic motifs. The kilims are usually large and rectangular, although long runners are also produced, and are articulated in a varied palette of generally bright colours. Corum items usually fall into the low-to-medium price bracket and are sometimes marketed under the name of the nearby town of Cankiri, which no longer produces kilims.

Dazkiri Town half-way between Afyon and Denizli in Turkey that produces very similar items to Denizli.

Denizli Town in western Turkey that is now a major centre for contemporary workshop kilims aimed at the export market, but also still produces some more authentic regional items. Contemporary workshop kilims from Denizli are indistinguishable from those made in the nearby weaving centres of Ushak and Esme. Denizli regional kilims are reasonably well made in a variety of mainly rectangular sizes and generally feature bold serrated medallions in fairly bright colours. They usually fall into the low-to-medium price bracket.

Drarab Generic name for good quality Iranian regional/workshop items that come in the low-to-medium price bracket.

El Jem Town in north-east Tunisia that produces kilims using the unusual technique of dyeing them (normally red) after they have been woven. Wool and cotton are used – the cotton resists the dye and the wool absorbs it, which results in the emergence of the pattern in direct relation to the position of the respective materials. Additional colours are produced by interweaving – using weft-faced patterning – additional sections of pre-dyed or natural wool and cotton. El Jem kilims are usually rectangular, small to medium in size, and fall into the low price bracket.

Elmadag Area in northern Turkey, meaning 'Apple Mountain', that produces good quality regional kilims of various sizes (although mainly rectangular). They are woven in fine slitweave and use mainly prayer-rug, banded and repeating 'crenellated diamond-shaped' medallion designs. The Elmadag palette is generally dominated by dark reds, blues, orange, black and brown, with white cotton highlights. Most Elmadag items fall into the low-to-medium price bracket.

Erzurum (pl 37) Town in north-east Turkey that makes good quality regional kilims, woven in slitweave, in a wide range of shapes and sizes. They frequently feature a variety of prayer-rug and tree-of-life designs – often set against a green or bluish green prayer field, with secondary shades of red, blue, orange, yellow – and use undyed brown wool for warps. Erzurum kilims usually fall into the low-to-medium and medium price brackets. Byburt, a village close by, produces very similar items, but they tend towards a slightly softer palette and the use of more naturalistic plant and floral motifs. The Erzurum region is also a centre for the production of Turkish Karabaghs.

Esme Town in western Turkey that produces both contemporary workshop kilims, made specifically for export, and some authentic regional items. Esme regional kilims are usually intricately decorated with a wide range of small geometric and symbolic motifs that surround and inwardly decorate larger medallion or amulet forms. The colours are normally bright, with softer pinks and greys. Most items are rectangular, woven in slitweave, and fall into the low-to-medium price bracket. Esme workshop kilims are very similar to those woven in Ushak.

Fars (pl 41) Province in southern Iran. A collective term for unattributed items (mainly Luri, Qashga'i and Khamseh) woven in the region.

Fethiye Popular tourist town on the Mediterranean coast of Turkey – built on the site of both the ancient Lydian city of Telmessus and the later Byzantine fortifications – that produces distinctive, medium quality kilims in two main compositions. The first are generally known as 'empty field' kilims and consist of a broad monochrome central section (usually woven in plainweave) sandwiched between two heavily decorated end sections that often contain large, interconnecting diamond motifs. The 'empty field' is normally red or pink, but a broader range of colours is used in the end sections and the overall palette tends towards being rather dark. The other main Fethiye composition employs the same range of end section motifs in an all-over format, without the intervention of an 'empty field'. They are both frequently woven in slitweave with supplementary weft wrapping, made in a variety of shapes and sizes and normally fall into the low price bracket.

Gafsa Large town in west central Tunisia noted for its brightly coloured regional/workshop kilims, woven in plainweave and dovetailing. They often feature human and animal figures, frequently offset by geometric forms, arranged in rows against an open or sparsely decorated field or incorporated into a banded format. Some medallion and panelled designs are also produced. Gafsa kilims are usually rectangular, small to medium in size, and fall into the low price bracket.

Garmsar Town near Veramin in Iran that produces very similar items which can sometimes

be distinguished by the inclusion of tiny 'daisy chain' or 'linked S-shaped' motifs on the end panels.

Gaziantep Town in south-east Turkey, near the Syrian border, formerly known as Antep and given the 'Gazi' prefix (which means 'defender of the faith') after holding out against French forces for nearly a year (1919–20) during the transitional period between the collapse of the Ottoman Empire and the founding of modern Turkey. Gaziantep no longer produces kilims, but old items still appear on the market. They are woven in slitweave (often in two halves) and usually feature a distinctive linked diamond motif – formed from a central diamond with two smaller diamonds attached to the top and bottom – used as an infill decoration in a variety of banded formats. Six-pointed stars, predominantly in white cotton, are also common.

Glaoua Region in the High Atlas Mountains, in Morocco, that lends its name to items woven by a number of indigenous Berber tribes. The Glaoua region is especially noted for pile rugs, but a number of very distinctive kilims are also produced. They are usually large and rectangular, and feature banded designs – in alternating plain and decorated sections – that employ a palette of predominantly black and white. They may be entirely flatwoven or may use alternating bands of kilim and pile.

Hamadan Large town in west central Iran, at the northern edge of Kurdistan, that is the marketing centre for items woven in dozens of villages within the immediate geographical region. Hamadan kilims are usually long and narrow or rectangular, woven in slitweave with supplementary weft insets and curved wefts, and normally feature variations on central-medallion and pole-medallion designs, articulated in a palette of mainly reds, deep pink, dark blue, yellow ochre and white. Most items are normally marketed collectively as Hamadans, although they may occasionally be sold under their individual name (e.g., Kasvin, etc.). They generally fall into the low price bracket.

Hanbel Generic name, meaning carpet, for good quality, low-to-medium priced, Moroccan regional/workshop kilims that are generally based on Berber weavings.

Harsin Town in the Hamadan region of Iran that is also a major producer of kilims, which are very similar in appearance, price and quality to those produced in Hamadan.

Kagizman Town near Kars in east Turkey that produces very similar items, which are frequently marketed as Kars.

Karapinar Village in the Konya district of southern Turkey noted for producing good quality regional kilims, employing prayer-rug, *saph* and stacked prayer-arch designs, that have a bold, rather primitive tribal character and appearance. Invariably woven in slit-weave, they are usually rectangular, employ pale ground colours, with darker shades for the motifs, and fall into the low-to-medium price bracket.

Kars Major town in eastern Turkey, near the Armenian border, that has a large Kurdish population. Kilims from the region show both a Kurdish and Caucasian influence (although the latter has gradually diminished since the Armenians were expelled during the early 20th century) and feature a variety of prayer-rug, repeating geometric and medallion compositions that vary in sophistication from simple tribal renditions of basic formats to complex, intricately articulated designs. They are invariably woven in slitweave, on distinctive natural brown woollen warps, in a wide variety of shapes and sizes; often unsuited to Western furnishing demands. Colours are traditionally dark and varied, although many recent items use a more limited, slightly paler palette of browns, pink, orange and white. Most Kars kilims fall into the low-to-medium price bracket.

Kayseria Major city, capital of Cappadocia (an early stronghold of Christendom in south central Turkey), that derives its present name from the Roman 'Caesarea', given to it in the 1st century AD in honour of Augustus Caesar. Kayseria is an important weaving centre for both regional and workshop kilims, and is especially noted for silk kilims, which are rarely, if ever, woven in other parts of Turkey.

Kayseria workshop kilims are generally fairly loosely woven (mainly in slitweave), employ rather garish colours (often red and black, sometimes fading to pink and grey) and are based on a wide range of traditional 'Kayseria' and other designs. However, some much finer examples (both in wool and silk) are also produced. Consequently, Kayseria workshop kilims may range in price from the low to the medium-to-high bracket.

Kayseria regional kilims are also woven in slitweave, either in wool or silk, but tend towards a more subdued palette of mainly reds, browns, orange, yellow and white. Designs are usually based either on panelled or banded (often broad or compartmentalized) compositions, featuring either repeating medallions – usually set against abundantly decorated fields – or extremely intricate all-over patternings of complex, interconnected geometric forms. The quality of the material and the weave varies considerably, so it is therefore extremely important to judge all Kayseria kilims on their individual merits. Woollen items can range from the low to medium price brackets, and silk items (especially older examples) from the medium to high.

Kecimuhsine Village near Konya, in southern Turkey, that produces *cicims* in a unique design based on a cypress tree intersecting stacked prayer arches. The palette is usually pale with pastel shades articulating the forms against a white or cream field. Kecimuhsine *cicims* are predominantly small and square. They are highly collectable and good examples often fall into the medium price bracket.

Keles Small town in the Uludag Mountains, in northern Turkey, that produces fairly coarse slitwoven kilims that possess strong tribal characteristics. They are often decorated with coloured tufts of wool (reputedly for good luck) and the Keles palette is dominated by rather subdued shades of reds, browns, blues and yellow. Small prayer rugs are especially common – although some larger items are produced in a variety of designs – and fall into the low-to-medium price bracket.

Kerman Capital of the Kerman Province, in south-eastern Iran, that gives its name to regional/tribal weavings produced in the region. The province's remoteness and inhospitable climate have for centuries made it a favourite place of exile for troublesome tribes, and today it is inhabited by Afshar, Qashga'i, Luri and other, mainly Turkic, tribesmen. Most of these tribesmen have now opted for a more settled lifestyle and have become integrated into the general population, although some nomadic and semi-nomadic tribal groups remain. Kerman kilims are therefore strongly influenced by diverse tribal weaving traditions (especially Afshar, Qashga'i and Luri) and feature a wide range of banded, medallion, all-over geometric, as well as other designs. They are produced in a variety of shapes and sizes, generally woven on cotton warps, using a weft-wrapping technique, and employ a frequently dark palette of reds, blues, orange, yellow ochre and white. Kerman kilims vary in price between the low and medium brackets.

Konya (pl 31) Large town in central Turkey that is now a centre for contemporary workshop production, although a significant number of authentic regional items are still made.

Konya workshop kilims are produced in a variety of sizes, shapes, colours and designs that are aimed specifically at the export market. Generally they are made in both standard and superior grades, which fall into the low and medium price brackets respectively.

Konya regional kilims (pl 31) are woven in slitweave or plainweave (sometimes with supplementary weft wrapping) in a variety of mainly rectangular sizes. They employ what is arguably the widest range of designs of any Turkish weaving group – although central medallions, repeating geometric motifs and a variety of complex all-over schemes are the most common – and their colour schemes are often equally diverse. In fact, their main distinguishing feature is often the sheer volume of motifs and intricate patterning of colour and form. Konya regional kilims usually fall into the medium or medium-to-high price brackets.

Labijar (pl 29) Generic name (meaning 'next to the canal or river') for a group of small villages, close to the Darya Safidi River in north central Afghanistan, inhabited by Uzbeks, Ersari Turkomen and, to a lesser extent, other tribal groups. Labijar kilims are tightly woven, usually in slitweave or double interlock, produced in a variety of sizes and shapes (including square) and feature mainly banded, zig-zag and panelled designs. The Labijar palette varies in intensity from fairly subdued to quite strong, but usually contains relatively harmonious shades of red, blue, deep orange, yellow and brown ochres, and white. Labijar kilims are sometimes divided into Ersari and Uzbek production, although this division can be quite arbitrary. Both generally fall into the low price bracket.

Ersari Labijars often feature squares with internal 'double-arrowhead' motifs, but it is not clear whether items with this design are woven exclusively by the Ersari Turkomen or whether the design is produced by weavers from different ethnic groups and merely linked with traditional Ersari designs.

Uzbek Labijars are more closely associated with panelled and inter-locking leaf (or 'Christmas Tree') designs, but, again, it is unclear whether this ethnic attribution is still valid or simply a recognition of the Uzbek design heritage.

Maimana Town in northern Afghanistan, capital of the Faryab Province, that is a major producer of regional/workshop kilims that usually feature a variety of mainly geometric motifs (usually diamond- or triangular-shaped) in all-over formats – sometimes with people, animals or domestic objects in the borders. The Maimana palette is dominated by strong reds, blues, oranges, brown and yellow ochres, with hints of green, white and occasionally other colours. They were originally associated with Uzbek weavers (Maimana being a generic name for all Uzbek items produced in the region). Now, though, they are also produced by Hazara, Tadjik, Aimaq, Turkoman and other tribal groups in the region – whose individual weaving heritages have largely fused into a more uniform 'Maimana' style – as well as in workshops in and around the town. Maimana kilims are woven, in a variety of sizes, using slitweave or double interlock, and normally fall into the low price bracket, although exceptional items from the region may be in the low-to-medium or medium categories.

Note Sutrangis are produced by the inmates of Maimana prison.

Almar, a village near Maimana, produces kilims that are very similar to Maimana kilims in colour, character and weave, but tend to employ large central medallions, often with internal and external 'hooked' motifs, rather than all-over geometric designs.

Malatya Town in the Tohmasuyu River Basin, near the eastern Taurus Mountains in eastern Turkey, consisting of one extraordinarily long main street. It is a centre for both contemporary workshop and regional weaving.

Malatya workshop kilims are produced in a wide variety of sizes and shapes, and employ both traditional Malatya and other, mainly Turkish and Caucasian, designs.

Malatya regional kilims are distinctively Kurdish in colour and design and items that employ one traditional Malatya composition – which consists of three or four linked (or pole) medallions – are often referred to as 'Rashwan' weavings after the Kurdish tribe of the same name. Banded and other medallion designs are also common. The Malatya palette is dominated by dark browns, reds, blue, green, orange, sienna, yellow ochre and white. Malatya regional kilims are generally rectangular, both large and small, and woven in slitweave or plainweave with supplementary weft wrapping. They usually fall into the low-to-medium and medium price brackets.

Manastir Generic name for regional kilims woven by Balkan expatriates, who settled in the Mihaliccik area of northern Turkey, distinguished by their bright, often sharply contrasting, primary colours and bold, sparsely decorated prayer-rug and repeating geometric (mainly serrated-diamond) designs. Manastir kilims are finely woven in slitweave, are normally small (although some larger sizes are made) and fall into the low-to-medium price bracket.

Meshed Principle city and marketing centre, in the Khorassan Province of eastern Iran, for Kurdish and other tribal weaving groups, whose weavings have to some degree fused into an overall regional style. The kilims produced in this region are generally of very good quality and are in the low-to-medium and medium price brackets. They are usually sold under their tribal affiliations (mainly Kurd, Afshar and Turkoman), but where an exact attribution is unclear they may be marketed simply as Meshed or Khorassan kilims.

Mukkur Town in southern Afghanistan that acts as a major marketing centre for kilims produced by the Kutchis and other indigenous tribal groups. Most items from the area are sold under their tribal names, but unattributed items may be marketed as Mukkurs.

Mut Village in the Taurus Mountains of southern Turkey, roughly halfway between Antalya and Adana, that acts as a centre for the nomadic and semi-nomadic Yoruk tribesmen. Mut kilims are distinctly tribal in appearance, and are frequently woven, in slitweave, with significant amounts of undyed wool, goat and horse hair. Designs are generally bold – often based on serrated or hexagonal medallions in a variety of interconnected or repeating designs – and are usually articulated in either bright or mellow shades of red, brown, pink, blue, yellow and white. Small and medium items (both rectangular and long and narrow) are commonly produced, and normally fall into the low or low-to-medium price bracket.

Nidge Town strategically placed on the ancient trade route between the southern coast and central and eastern Turkey, noted for fine quality kilims that often feature serrated hexagonal motifs in complex, repeating formats. They are similar to items woven in Konya and are often marketed as such (or as Kars).

Obruk (pl 37) Town in south central Turkey renowned for its finely woven prayer rugs (usually in slitweave with extensive supplementary weft wrapping), frequently inwardly decorated with variations on the tree-of-life format. Obruk also produces *cicims*, which often feature geometric forms, especially interconnecting diamonds, as well as other – mainly medallion and banded – designs. The Obruk palette varies from bright to dark, usually with a dominance of reds and blues, with supplementary yellow, orange and white. Obruk kilims are made in a variety of sizes and shapes, and normally fall into the low-to-medium price bracket.

Oudref Area in northern Tunisia noted for saddle blankets (*bost*) and other textile artefacts. Kilims are produced, in wool and cotton, using plainweave and weft-faced patterning, often featuring tiny geometric motifs in either repeating and all-over formats or banded designs. Colours vary, but white cotton is frequently used to highlight the design. Most Oudref kilims are rectangular, small to medium in size, and fall into the low-to-medium price bracket.

Matmata kilims and textile artefacts are produced in a troglodyte town, in southern Tunisia, and are very similar in colour, design and structure to those woven in Oudref, although the use of white cotton is not as dominant.

Oudzem (pl 13) Generic name for standard quality Moroccan workshop kilims – usually woven in a mixture of plainweave, tapestry weave and supplementary floating wefts (mainly white cotton) that often feature simple animal, floral or geometric and 'village' motifs, in a varied palette of cream, blue, green, with some reds and other supplementary colours. They are aimed at the (mainly French) tourist and wider export markets and usually fall into the low price bracket.

Qala-i-Nau Small town, near Herat in north-western Afghanistan, inhabited by Hazara Aimaq and other tribal groups who produce good quality regional/tribal kilims that are similar in character and appearance to items woven by other Chahar Aimaq tribes. Intricately patterned banded designs are common, although different 'Belouch-type' compositions are found (including semi-pile items). The Qala-i-Nau palette often includes quite mellow shades of cherry red and gold. The name 'Qala-i-Nau' is normally used as a generic term for items produced both in the town itself and in the neighbouring village of Laghari and the surrounding area, populated by nomadic and semi-nomadic tribes, who also produce good quality *khorjin* and other bags and artefacts. Most Qala-i-Nau items fall into the low-to-medium price bracket.

Redeyef Village in Tunisia close to the Algerian border that produces kilims that are very similar to those woven in Gafsa, except that they use supplementary weft-faced patterning (rather than dovetailing). Sometimes contain cotton and feature additional designs – mainly all-over geometric motifs of various sizes set within a large central compartment. They usually fall into the low price bracket.

Reyhanli Village in southern Turkey that produced, until the early 20th century, some of the very finest Anatolian kilims. They often feature central medallions, frequently with 'leaf and vine' meanders in the borders, and employ a dark palette of mainly reds, blues and greens, with contrasting white (often cotton). Old Reyhanli kilims are highly collectable and range in price between the medium and high categories.

Sar-i-Pul (pl 27) Town in north central Afghanistan, on the fringes of the Hindu Kush Mountains, inhabited by large numbers of Hazara Aimaqs, Uzbeks, Pathans and other tribal groups, which is associated with the production of regional/tribal kilims that conform to one extremely distinctive style. They are generally quite finely woven (normally using weft-faced plainweave and weft-faced patterning) in banded formats that are distinguished by their extensive use of broad monochrome sections, normally in cream or white, separated by smaller bands of coloured patterning. These kilims are usually associated with the Hazara – although Uzbeks weave similar items – and kilims woven in the region that feature other designs are predominantly marketed under their tribal name (Uzbek, etc.). Sar-i-Pul kilims usually fall into the low-to-medium price bracket.

Sarkisla Small town near Sivas in Turkey that produces similar items that are often marketed as Sivas. However, Sarkisla kilims are generally more loosely woven, employ a darker palette and feature repeating hexagonal or hooked diamond forms.

Sarkoy (pl 35) Generic name for regional/workshop kilims produced in European Turkey (Thrace) and Bulgaria that often have fairly naturalistic tree-of-life, floral, bird and 'leaf and vine' motifs. They are generally extremely finely woven – in slitweave with some curvilinear supplementary weft wrapping or insertion – and employ a rich, often slightly dark palette of mainly red, blue and green, with contrasting yellow and white. Sarkoy kilims are produced in a variety of sizes and shapes, and normally fall into the medium price bracket. They are sometimes marketed under other names, e.g., Pirot, Gocmen.

Sarmayie Generic name for regional/tribal kilims woven by Chahar Aimaq tribesmen, who inhabit the area in and around the town of Charchangan, in west central Afghanistan. Sarmayie kilims usually feature banded compositions – often with diamond-shaped inner decorations – and employ a soft palette of browns, yellows, burnt orange and brick red. They are very similar in structure to other Chahar Aimaq weavings and normally fall into the low-to-medium price bracket.

Senneh or Senna (pl 21) City, now called Sanandaj, capital of Kurdistan, in western Iran, that produces extremely fine quality regional/workshop kilims. They usually feature small flowers or *botehs* arranged in an all-over, repeating format – either across the entire field or within skeletal medallions on variegated grounds. The Senneh palette is frequently red and blue, with white, yellow ochre and green secondary colours, and the overall tone may be either dark or subdued. Most kilims are relatively small and rectangular, although some larger or squarer items are also made, and invariably woven in very fine slitweave with supplementary weft inserts and curved wefts. Senneh weavings may lack some of the tribal vivacity of other kilims from Kurdistan, but they are among the best quality of all contemporary items on the market today and usually fall into the medium price bracket.

Serhandi Generic term for good quality kilims from the Maimana region of Afghanistan. They are finely woven, usually in dovetailing and double interlock, and have a slightly softer palette, but are otherwise very similar to standard Maimana kilims.

Shiraz Large town in the Fars Province of southern Iran that acts as the main marketing centre for Qashga'i, Luri, Khamseh and other nomadic tribes. The town also produces regional/workshop kilims that are based on Qashga'i – and to a lesser extent – other local nomadic weavings, although Shiraz kilims are generally produced in shapes and sizes that are more compatible with Western furnishing requirements. Quality varies considerably – at best, Shiraz kilims are well made, extremely attractive and compare favourably with authentic nomadic items, however, a significant number of shoddier, much less attractive items are also produced. It is therefore extremely important to judge all Shiraz (or Qashga'i) kilims on their individual merits, rather than rely on the reputation of the weaving group. This is especially important as it is common practice among some dealers to treat the two names as interchangeable, especially if there is no clear indication as to whether an individual item was made by the nomadic Qashga'i or settled weavers of diverse tribal origins in one of the numerous workshops in and around Shiraz. The price of Shiraz kilims reflects their varying quality and ranges from the low to low-to-medium bracket.

Sidi Bou Zid Town in northern Tunisia noted for producing kilims, woven in plainweave and dovetailing, that are often based on pile rug designs. Medallions, usually set against open or sparsely decorated grounds, are common and frequently articulated in a bright and varied palette, often dominated by reds. Sidi Bou Zid kilims are predominantly rectangular, medium sized, and fall into the low price bracket.

Sinan Village near Malatya in eastern Turkey noted for small kilims, woven with supplementary white cotton and metallic threads, that are distinctly tribal in appearance. They often employ prayer-rug and sparsely decorated all-over designs in dark red, blue, black, white and undyed wool.

Sivas Large town in east central Turkey that was once the capital of Armenia Minor and an important point on the ancient trade routes to Iran, Iraq and the Caucasus. It has a mixed Turkic and Kurdish population, and both influences are evident in its kilims, which are similar in character and appearance to those from other parts of eastern Turkey. They are, however, generally lighter in colour with a predominance of bright red, orange, pale green, viridian, cream, white and pale yellow and brown ochres. Small prayer rugs and to a lesser extent *saphs*, employing a variety of small floral, geometric and other infill motifs, are common. Larger items, frequently based on central or repeating medallions or other large geometric forms, are also produced. Sivas kilims are generally of good quality, finely woven – using slitweave, plainweave and supplementary weft wrapping – and are within the medium price bracket. Some *cicims* are also made.

Sivrihisar Town roughly halfway between Ankara and Afyon in central Turkey, whose name translates as 'pinnacled castle', noted for kilims that employ a series of vertically stacked, angular prayer arches (or sections of battlement) known as the *bacali* or chimney pot design. *Elibelinde* designs are also common. Sivrihisar kilims are usually quite finely woven, in slitweave, employ a bright and varied palette, and fall into the low-to-medium price bracket.

Talish Town in north-west Iran, near Rasht on the Caspian Sea, noted for good quality regional kilims that are usually based on all-over and repeating stepped diamonds or medallions in a varied palette of strong, contrasting colours. They are normally long and narrow, quite finely woven, in slitweave (often using undyed woollen wefts), and fall into the low price bracket.

Taznakht and Klenifra Villages in Morocco inhabited by settled Berber tribesmen. Taznakht kilims are mainly long and narrow, sometimes with supplementary pile, and are of very good quality. Klenifra kilims are similar to Zaiane weavings.

Tiffelt Generic name for superior quality Moroccan workshop kilims – usually quite finely woven in a mixture of plainweave, tapestry weave and floating wefts, sometimes in silk or mercerized cotton (art silk) – that feature a variety of highly detailed, mainly geometric, patternings in a range of primarily all-over and panelled (or compartmentalized) formats. The Tiffelt palette is primarily composed of cream, silver, reds and black, with a range of supplementary colours. They are produced in a wide variety of sizes and shapes, and usually fall into the low-to-medium and medium price brackets.

Ushak (pl 9) Town in western Turkey that is now one of the major centres for contemporary workshop kilims woven primarily for the export market, but that also produces some more authentic regional items.

Ushak workshop kilims (pl 9) are produced in standard and superior grades in a wide variety of designs, colour schemes, sizes and shapes, and are largely indistinguishable from those produced in the neighbouring towns of Denizli and Esme.

Ushak regional kilims are usually fairly large, square and woven in loose slitweave. They often feature central medallions, set against open or sparsely decorated grounds, and employ a palette of red (often used as a ground colour), blue, green, yellow, mauve, black and white. They normally fall into the low-to-medium price bracket.

Van (pl 5) Major town in the remote, mountainous region of eastern Turkey, situated a few miles south-east of Lake Van, close to the Armenian border. The town not only produces its own regional kilims, but also acts as an important marketing centre for the mainly Kurdish tribes in the region. Van kilims are generally square or rectangular, medium sized and woven (often in two halves) in fairly tight slitweave, with occasional additions of metallic and synthetic thread. The main compositions are based on large 'hooked' or 'crenellated' diamonds (often separated by narrow bands) or on more traditional banded designs employing a variety of small geometric infill motifs. The Van palette is invariably dark, with a predominance of red, blue, brown and occasionally green, offset by white and yellow ochre traceries and highlights. The two largest and most important local Kurdish tribes are the Herki and the Hartushi, both of whom produce kilims that may be marketed under their tribal names or collectively as Vans.

Hartushi kilims are extremely difficult to distinguish from other items produced in and around Van, as well as from those woven by their kinsmen across the border in Iraq, and are therefore usually marketed as either Van or simply Kurdish kilims. Similarly, items woven in Iraq by Hartushi or other Kurdish tribesmen may be also sold as Van kilims.

Herki kilims (pl 5) are very similar to Hartushi and other Van kilims, but often employ a weft-wrapping technique.

Veramin (pl 30) Ancient city, near Tehran in north central Iran, that produces extremely good quality regional kilims, usually large and rectangular, woven in very fine slitweave with occasional contour banding (on cotton or sometimes woollen warps), in a number of mainly all-over, repeating geometric or banded designs. The individual motifs vary considerably, but they are usually small and sharply serrated, often within a series of smaller, different-coloured inner motifs. They are frequently arranged in diagonal rows or as zig-zag diamonds, with each row employing sharply contrasting colours (mainly red, blue, green, yellow, orange and white), although older items often have a more subdued and harmonious colour scheme. One famous design associated with Veramin – although it is also produced by the Qashga'i and some other Iranian weaving groups – is the 'eye-dazzler' kilim (pl 30) which has rows of small, contrastingly coloured, sharply serrated motifs in concentrically expanding diamond zig-zags radiating across the entire field. The visual effect is one of shimmering or 'dazzling' at the junctions between the different-coloured motifs – not dissimilar to that produced by Western 'Op Artists'. Bags, *soufrehs* and *rukorssis* are also woven and, in common with Veramin kilims, usually fall into the low-to-medium or medium price range.

Zarand Generic name given to good quality regional kilims produced in the small towns of Zarand, Qazvin and Saveh, in north central Iran. They are usually long and narrow, finely woven on cotton warps – using slitweave with supplementary weft inserts and curved wefts – and feature a variety of all-over, repeating stylized floral (or geometric) patterns and stepped diamonds or pole medallions. The Zarand palette varies between soft, almost pastel browns, blues, oranges and yellow ochre, and the occasional use of much brighter primary shades. They are strongly influenced by the local Shahsavan and to a lesser extent Kurdish tribesmen. Kilims from Zarand, Qazvin and Saveh are normally marketed under the collective title of Zarands – although they may sometimes be sold under the names of the individual towns – and fall into the low-to-medium price bracket.

Index